TED MENTEN
TEDDY BEAR STUDIO

A Step-By-Step Guide to Creating
Your Own One-of-a-Kind Artist Teddy Bear

RUNNING PRESS
PHILADELPHIA • LONDON

9   8   7   6   5 4   3   2   1
Digit on the right indicates the number of this printing

Library of Congress Cataloging-in-Publication Number 2001094115

ISBN 0-7624-1235-6

Photography, art, and interior design by Ted Menten
Edited by Greg Jones
Computer graphic design by Brian Pinkley
Typography: Tempus Sans

This book may be ordered by mail from the publisher.
Please include $2.50 for postage and handling.
But try your bookstore first!

Running Press Book Publishers
125 South Twenty-second Street
Philadelphia, Pennsylvania 19103-4399

Visit us on the web!
www.runningpress.com

CONTENTS

The person who creates a TeddyBear creates love.
The person who adopts a TeddyBear perpetuates it.

A TEDDY TALE

Two of my favorite words are *serendipity* and *synchronicity*. I like them because they sound amusing, even whimsical. And, in some way, they are just that.

Serendipity comes from the Persian fairy tale *The Three Princes* which first appeared in 1754. The dictionary defines it as: "the faculty or phenomenon of finding valuable or agreeable things not sought for."

Synchronicity appeared a bit later, in 1889, and the dictionary defines it as: "the coincidental occurrence of events and especially psychic events (as similar thoughts in widely separated persons or a mental image of an unexpected event before it happens) that seem related but are not explained by conventional mechanisms of causality."

This is the story of the Teddy Bear, and I believe it contains both serendipity and synchronicity—and a very large tablespoon of love.

SERENDIPITY AND SYNCHRONICITY AND A MOMENT IN TIME

The sun broke through the clouds and promised another perfect autumn day. The bright crimson and gold leaves floated gently to the ground in their tiny dance of death. The lawn of the White House was speckled with leaves as President Theodore Roosevelt pondered the position he might be forced to take in a border dispute between Mississippi and Louisiana. The only bright spot in that prospect was that, if he went down there in person, he might get in a little hunting....

Richard Steiff paced around his aunt's workroom passionately trying to persuade her to make a toy bear based on his drawings. Her delightful toy elephants were extremely popular and Richard was sure that a toy bear would be popular as well. Unconvinced, but at heart a loving aunt, Margarette wheeled her chair over to the sewing table and began to draft a pattern for the first toy bear....

Clifford Berryman woke to another day and another deadline for a cartoon....

And destiny smiled; maybe even chuckled.

The President made the decision to go to Mississippi in person, settle the boundary dispute, and get in a little hunting. The divergent group of White House staff and the President's hunting buddies set off on a journey that would, within a week, change the lives of all concerned.

In the political arena, fact and fiction are strange bedfellows. Reporters in those days were not much different from reporters today—they wanted a good story and, in this case, it wasn't the boundary dispute. There are many different versions of what transpired next, but the basic story is this:
After several days of tracking, the prospects of any substantial quarry faded and the President was clearly disappointed. In an effort to cheer him up, the trackers found a bear for him to shoot. Versions differ here as to whether it was a baby cub or a tired, older bear. The bear was tied to a tree and the President was invited to take his best shot. President Roosevelt refused to shoot the bear, saying his children would never forgive him if he did.

This is the *moment*. This is Washington crossing the Delaware. This is Newton getting conked on the head with an apple. This is Ben Franklin in the lightning storm.

A few days later, on the morning of November 16, 1902, Clifford K. Berryman approached his drawing table with a smile—he had a cartoon to draw! And draw it he did, not realizing that with each pen-stroke his life was changing in a way he could never have imagined.

Later that day the President opened *The Washington Post* and laughed out loud. There, on the editorial page, was Berryman's cartoon titled "Drawing the Line in Mississippi." In the cartoon, Roosevelt is decked out in full hunting gear, rifle in hand. He stands, legs firmly planted apart, with a grim expression on his face, his outstretched arm signaling a firm "No." The second *moment* was recorded.

DRAWING THE LINE IN MISSISSIPPI

A few days later, Richard Steiff sat beside his aunt holding the toy bear she had created from his drawings, and the third *moment* occurred.

But, like all watershed moments, there was another moment in this story that could have changed everything. (What if Washington couldn't find a boat? What if Newton's apple never fell? What if Franklin had decided he didn't want to get wet in the rain?)

A few months after these three important moments had occurred, something else happened that might have rendered them meaningless.

At the 1903 Leipzig Fair, the Steiff family presented their line of stuffed toys to generally enthusiastic reviews.

But the tiny toy bear was not appreciated at all and seemed doomed to fall by the wayside.

However, an American toy buyer from the George Borgfelt Company in New York City felt that the toy bear had promise and ordered three thousand bears to be shipped immediately.

It was a small beginning for the many millions of Steiff bears that would soon follow.

By 1906 the toy bear was declared a "craze" by *Playthings*, the official trade publication of the toy industry. In a long article published that year and titled "The Plush Craze," it was stated that one New York toy store had reported sales of sixty-thousand teddy bears.

If William Shakespeare were writing this tale, he might have penned this closing phrase, "Serendipity and synchronicity, thy name is Teddy Bear."

If beauty is in the eyes of the beholder, every bear will find a home.

INTRODUCTION

Welcome to my teddy bear studio. If you were actually sitting here with me you would see a large room with tall windows facing a terrace that looks out over the Manhattan skyline, including the Empire State Building. The sun streams in after two in the afternoon and puts a golden glow on the fur of the hundreds of Teddys that line the shelves of the side wall. Close to the terrace windows is a giant worktable that once served as a dining table for twelve. Now it is used to nourish my creative spirit and my Teddy Bear soul.

Nearby, baskets are filled with a variety of fur pieces, and boxes of fabric line the far wall and have labels reading "Laura Ashley type prints" or "Christmas pattern prints." Other smaller boxes contain ribbons and lace trims, and still smaller boxes hold buttons and glass eyes.

My sewing machine (one of many) is an old Singer from the 1960s that I bought when I started designing toys professionally. It came with free lessons, but after the first day the teacher expelled me from class because I couldn't learn to thread my needle properly. My friend, Pat, taught me to sew between swigs of fine Irish whiskey that kept us both relaxed during my sessions of out-and-out stupidity.

Finally, I learned to sew. And over the years I've finally learned to thread my machine and backstitch like a professional. On the other hand, zigzagging is still something of a mystery. Joking aside, my point is that even the most experienced professional started out with a blank stare and five thumbs on each hand. I look back with humor on those days but, hopefully, the experience has made me a much more understanding and compassionate instructor.

FAILING ON THE ROAD TO SUCCESS

Here is my motto: "There are no lessons in success. All the lessons are in failure." Think about it. If you do something correctly, that's it. But if you make a mistake—if you blunder, stumble, and fall—then you must learn how to overcome that failure to become successful. That in itself is a learned lesson, but I've discovered that one lesson learned from a failure usually yields even more information.

I've taught hundreds of classes and thousands of students all over the world. I teach them all to fail as often as possible. Failing means you took a risk, and that always leads to better, more creative solutions. If one of my students screws up, they raise their hand and tell their story. I often have the answer, but more often than not other students have had the same problem and solved it with alternate solutions. Now one mistake has yielded a dozen solutions and we are all wiser for it—including me. Almost everything I know I learned from my mistakes and my student's solutions.

What I learned is that the so-called HOW-TO of life is really the HOW-YOU-MIGHT of life because there are many different roads to success. And speaking of roads, the single most important thing to remember on this adventure into bear making is the importance of the journey itself. The Teddy Bear is simply where you are going—the final destination. Making the bear is the journey and we must take time to enjoy every step along the way. We need to breath in the air of creation and smell the fragrance of both failure and success. This is the great adventure, with myriad twists and turns, with secrets revealed, and wonders experienced. On this journey we don't think about the result, but the process. The bear will happen as a result of a well traveled exploration into its creation.

Welcome to my studio. Join me and let us begin this delightful and wondrous excursion into the wonder-filled world of Teddy Bears.

HOW-TO, NOT-TO, AND HOW-YOU-MIGHT

There are lots of wonderful how-to books published every year and I try to read as many of them as possible. They all do a wonderful job of taking the reader by the hand and leading them step-by-step through the process of creativity. But are they really teaching, or even encouraging, creative thinking? If you are simply following the instructions step-by-step, how creative is that? We all have that creative spark inside us just waiting to ignite and explode into something marvelous and original and totally new and different.

So I decided that instead of teaching my students "how-to," I decided to teach them "how-you-might." Or, how-to "not-to." The basic not-to was not-to just make a bear from one of the patterns I provided. I showed them how-you-might change those basic patterns into something new and original. I showed them how-you-might alter and customize it to become an expression of your own. Ladies often alter a dress pattern or do a makeover of an old one. Men customize their cars or motorcycles to make them uniquely their own.

And that's what this book will teach you to do when creating your own Teddy Bear.

A stitch in time saves nine, but a stitch in a bear saves stuffing.

THE MAGICAL TOOLBOX

There are as many different tools used to make Teddy Bears as there are bearmakers. Every time I teach a class I learn that someone has discovered a new tool or technique to make the work better and/or easier.

Basically, there are just a few things that you will absolutely need, so I'll deal with them first. Unless you intend to hand-sew your bear you'll need a sewing machine. If you don't have one and are thinking about buying one for bearmaking, here are some tips. Often times an older, rebuilt machine is as good as, or better than, a new machine. Working with fur presents several problems, and one of them is dust and fur fragments that will get into everything. For that reason an electronic machine might not be a good choice. You want a machine that is easy to clean and maintain. Another factor is the pressure foot that must hold the fur pieces tightly together to be sewn properly. Some modern machines have automatic, self-adjusting systems that misread the thickness of the fur and do not stitch tightly enough. You only need to be able to straight-sew, backstitch, and zigzag to make a Teddy Bear.

Besides a basic sewing machine you'll need some basic sewing thread. You will need a variety of needles for hand sewing. A selection of scissors, each for a particular purpose, is essential. Paper scissors for cutting patterns and fabric scissors for cutting fur–and never the twain shall meet! Buy scissors for specific use and only use them for that purpose. You'll need straight pins for pinning and you'll need some combs and brushes.

Art supplies like pattern paper, ruler, and permanent ink felt-tip markers are also basic needs.

Stuffing tools vary from those commercially designed for stuffing, to screw drivers, chop sticks, and long-handled wooden spoons. This area of choice is diverse enough to fill a book of its own.

This is a basic group of tools to get you started but, in time, you'll discover a host of others that will fill your toolbox to overflowing.

BECKY

IMAGINING AND IMAGING

The first thing we do is imagine the bear you want to create. Boy or girl? Young or old? Tall or short? Chubby or thin? Dressed or undressed? Once you have decided on the basic characteristics of your bear we move ahead to imaging.

Imaging means that you close your eyes and think of your bear until you can completely visualize him, or her, in your mind's eye. Keep thinking and visualizing until the clouds part and the completed bear is clearly revealed. Focus on every detail and then write it down. Here is an example of an imagined and imaged bear:

The designer says, "Her name will be 'Betsy' and she's a young, chubby bear dressed in rompers and holding a basket of flowers from her garden. She has light brown curly fur and her paw pads are made of a lighter shade of tan Ultra Suede. She has a dark brown nose and black, shoe-button eyes that are close set and a bit innocent looking. She wears a matching ribbon bow in her hair."

I certainly can see that bear very clearly. It turns out that Betsy is really a Teddy Bear version of the designer's daughter when she was six years old. She has a color photograph for reference. Photographs provide excellent reference for creating bears. So do children's picture books.

With the bear clearly imaged in your mind, you now must make a list of things to make and things to find.

For Betsy we will need:
Brown curly fur
Tan Ultra Suede
Dark brown embroidery thread
Black shoe-button eyes
Floral cotton fabric for rompers
Basket of flowers

We'll also need to decide if Betsy's arm will be bent in order to carry the basket over it or remain straight so she can carry the basket with her paw.

After we have completed the imaging, made our list, and collected the various items we'll need to create Betsy, we are ready to make a pattern.

TeddyBears are a dreamer's best friend.

SAY HELLO TO ADAM AND EVE

Over the years, my students and I have created thousands of unique Teddy Bears beginning with the ADAM and EVE templates as their parents or ancestors (these templates are included at the end of this book). There is often a strong family resemblance between the offspring, but there are just as many that seem to spring forth from an entirely unique Genesis. Just as we humans are as uniquely different as we are basically alike. Our Teddy Bears will be a reflection of those two factors—the similarity of species and the specific uniqueness of each individual. Even in the human species, not even so-called identical twins are absolutely alike in every detail. So even two bears made from the same pattern and made of the same fur will not be exactly alike. Not even so-called mass manufactured bears are so alike as to be devoid of charming, individual differences.

While ADAM and EVE are based on the very simple principle that boys are generally taller than girls, the sexism ends there. Teddy Bears of any persuasion can be made from either pattern or mixture of pattern pieces. What is important is to visualize your specific bear and then choose the pattern pieces that will best express that bear in your imagination.

Once, while teaching a class in Canada, I asked the students to do a little rough drawing of the bear they had in mind. As I walked around the room I saw little girl bears and ballerina bears and Santa bears and several chubby cuddle bears. One lady had drawn a sitting bear in profile that had an enormous belly. It was one of the fattest bears I'd ever seen. "Is that bear pregnant?" I asked. "Oh, my, no," the artist replied, "she's going to be a pin cushion."

Sure enough, when the bear was finished, it was a wonderful pincushion bear with a tummy filled with fine sand to sharpen the needles and weigh down the Teddy Bear in a seated position beside her sewing machine.

SELECTING THE BASIC PATTERNS

There are two basic patterns. One female, EVE, and one male, ADAM.

Actually, that is just na easy way to differentiate between their characteristics.

Eventually you will mix and match patterns from both and create either male and female bears or just plain unisex bears of neither persuasion.

My friend Nancy has only one bear and she calls it "William or Mary depending." Depending on the outfit of the day and the event they are attending together.

The EVE pattern has a shorter nose, shorter body, and shorter arms and legs—but that could easily describe a small boy bear as well.

The ADAM pattern has a longer nose, longer body, and longer arms and legs; this pattern could also be a teen-age boy or girl.

When we look at the basic patterns you'll see that the different versions of heads, bodies, legs, and arms provide you with an unlimited set of variations.

And that's before you choose a style of ears!

BASIC EVE PATTERN

This is the basic A pattern. The head, body, arms, and legs are all created from the basic A pattern pieces with no modifications.

BASIC ADAM PATTERN

This is the basic B pattern. The head, body, arms, and legs are all created from the basic B pattern pieces with no modifications.

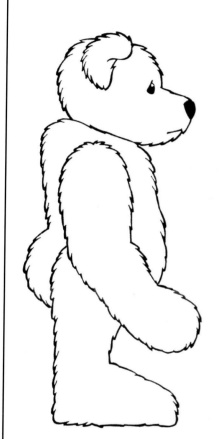

TIMELESS TEDDY

This Timeless Teddy is created
with the A head pattern and
the A body and leg patterns.
The arms are created with the
B pattern to create the look of
the original, old-fashioned
Teddy Bear we call a classic.

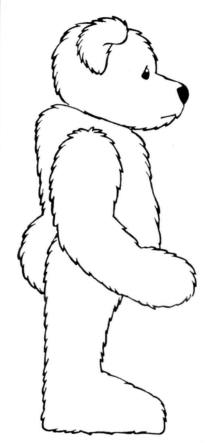

TEEN-AGE TEDDY

This Teen-age Teddy is made
from the B head pattern and
the B body and leg patterns.
The arms are created with
the A patttern.
This style bear is referred to
as a 'doll bear' because it
resembles the style and
proportion of a toddler doll.

GERMAN-STYLE TEDDY

This German-style Teddy is
created with the B head, body,
and arm patterns. The legs are
created from the A pattern.
This design creates the look of
the early German bears that
had longer noses, arms, and
bodies.

CREATING A FAMILY OF TEDDY BEARS

Working with the basic ADAM or EVE patterns you can create an entire family of Teddy Bears ranging from a baby, to a toddler, to a teen, to an adult, and finally, to a high-fashion model bear.

On each pattern piece you will see a dotted cut line. If you want to add or subtract height you must cut this line first.

After you have cut the pattern piece you can decide just the right amount of space to be taken out or added in.

To shorten the pattern piece, just slip one half slightly behind the other and glue or tape the two pieces together.

To lengthen the pattern piece, insert a length of pattern paper between the cut pattern pieces and tape them together.

When altering the arm pieces be careful to adjust both the back and front exactly the same way so that they will fit together perfectly when sewn.

Adding a neck to the head is not very complicated but you must remember to add the same amount to both left and right pattern pieces as well as the back of the center gusset pattern piece.

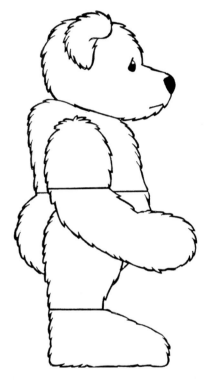

BABY BEAR

This Baby Bear is created by using the basic A pattern.
No alteration has been made to the head pattern.
About one half inch has been removed from the body, arm, and leg patterns to shorten the height of the bear.

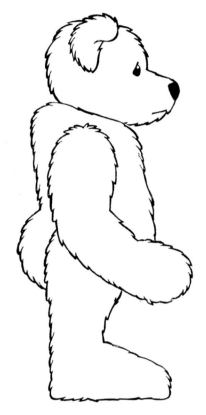

TODDLER BEAR

This Toddler Bear is created by using the basic A pattern. The head, body, arms, and legs are all made from the basic A pattern pieces with no modifications.

TEEN-AGE BEAR

This Teen Bear is created by using the A head, body, and arm patterns without any modifications. The legs are created from the B pattern without any modification.

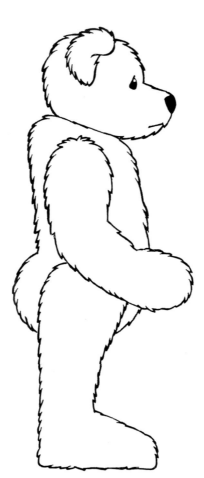

ADULT BEAR

This Adult Bear is created by using the A head and arm patterns without modification. The body and legs are made from the B pattern pieces without any modification.

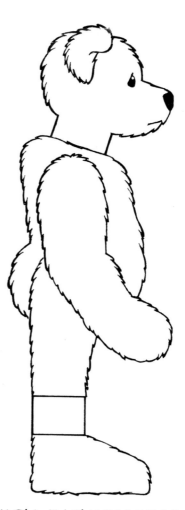

HIGH-FASHION BEAR

This Fashion Bear is created by using the B pattern pieces for the body and arms without any modifications.
The basic A head pattern has been modified to include a one-inch longer neck.
The B pattern legs have been modified by adding two inches to the length.

REDESIGNING THE HEAD PATTERNS

No design element is more important than creating a wonderful head for your Teddy Bear.

Many artists struggle for years to come up with a special and unique design that will set their creations apart from the others. This is by no means an easy task, but trial and error will ultimately reward you with a bear design in your own personal style.

Altering head patterns can take many directions. You can change the profile, alter the length and width of the nose or change the shape and placement of the ears.

There are techniques to create a two-tone face and even a trick or two to alter the shape of the head. All of these varied elements contribute to making your bear different from the others, even though you are starting with the same basic set of head patterns.

Keep in mind that any change made in the profile of the head must also be made to the center gusset so that all of the pieces will fit perfectly.

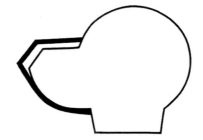

To change the design of the basic head you must begin with the profile. Even subtle differences can make a significant change in the bear's appearance. Raising the bridge of the nose and adding a bit of chin is a good first step.

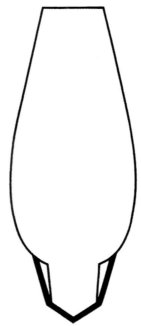

Keep in mind that the smallest change in the profile must be reflected in the center gusset pattern as well. In this design, only the width of the bridge of the nose must be changed to fit the new profile.

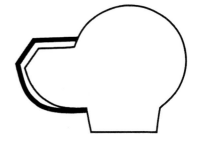

This more dramatic nose design appears to be a lot more complicated but in reality it is not. Once again the profile is altered to give the bear a larger nose and a higher forehead.

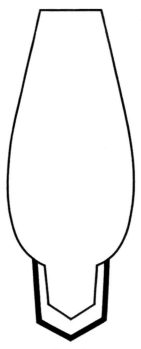

Basically, the redesign of the center gusset must reflect the change in the profile. The length of the bridge of the nose and the nose tip must match the new profile.

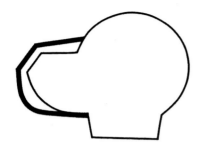

This head design will create a pointed nose design as well as a very wide nose bridge at the top of the nose. Many artists use this type of pattern if they intend to soft-sculpt the nose and create deep-set eyes.

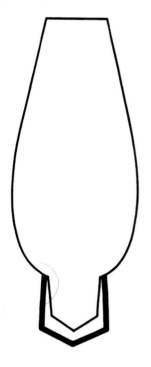

Once again, all of the pieces must be created to fit exactly into each other so that they will fit perfectly when sewn together.

TWO-COLOR AND TWO-PIECE PROFILES

Creating a two-color head isn't all that complicated, but it takes a bit of patience when it comes to sewing all the pieces together. At times it almost seems like making a fur patchwork quilt.

Looking at the top illustration on the right, you see the nose divided at two points and the head divided at two points. This is your basic starting point.

If you just want to have a different color nose on your bear, just cut the basic pattern along the line from the bridge of the nose to the bottom of the chin. Add a one-quarter inch seam allowance and sew the pieces together. Remember also to cut the center gusset pattern at the bridge of the nose, add seam allowance and sew together.

If you want a different-colored face for your bear, you can cut the basic head profile in the center, add seam allowance, and sew together. Do the same to the gusset.

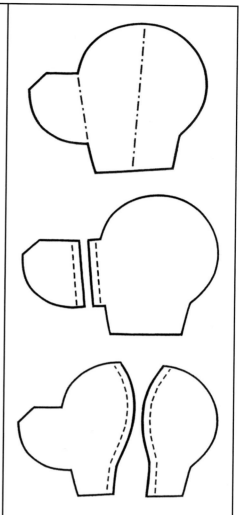

To create a fatter face you can add a slight curve to the sides of the pattern.

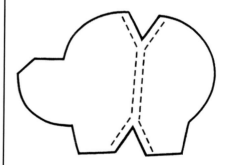

If you just want a fatter one-color head, you can fake the curves with two V-shaped darts.

CHANGING THE PATTERN PROFILE

There are several ways to change the size and shape of your Teddy Bear design without creating a totally new set of patterns. The first of these is rearranging pattern pieces to create a variety of different-sized bears. Another way is to shorten and lengthen the pattern pieces. And still another involves changing the profile of the various pieces.

When changing the profile of a pattern piece the most important rule is: ALWAYS CHANGE THE SEWING LINE FIRST. Whenever you redesign a pattern, you must always work with the sewing line and add the cutting line only after you are satisfied with the new shape of the sewing line.

The profile of the arms and legs are the easiest to change as they only involve two pieces. Changing a head pattern involves altering three pieces—the two profiles and the center gusset. Changing a body pattern can involve a simple profile alteration or the creation of a four-part body that has been altered front and back or side to side.

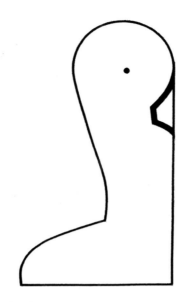

The leg pattern can be created in one or two pieces. The one piece pattern folds over to create the profile. Always redesign on the sewing line indicated on the pattern.

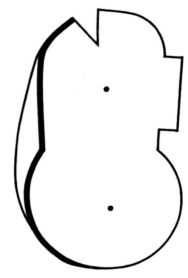

Body patterns can be altered by simply changing the front of the pattern. This shape is referred to as a "light bulb."

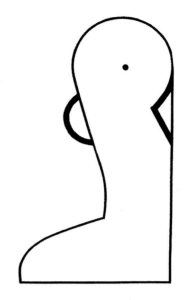

This pattern has had a knee added to the front of the leg —and the back of the knee indented—to add character to the shape of the leg.

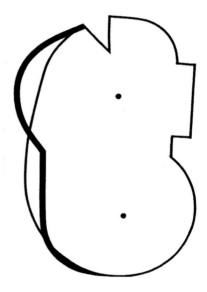

This shape gives the bear a bigger chest and a smaller waist and hips. This shape is referred toas the "super hero."

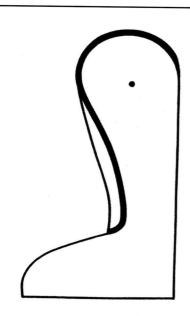

To create a slimmer leg just narrow the profile of the front of the leg below the disk area. Be careful not to narrow the ankle too much and weaken it.

This design creates a softer knee shape that adds character without creating a leg design that is too knobby-kneed.

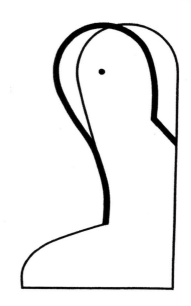

This leaning-forward shape leg demonstrates that even with a single-piece folded pattern you can create unusual shapes.

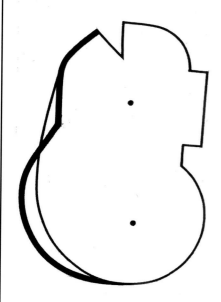

This reshaping of the front of the pattern will give your bear a big pot belly. This design is referred to as the "Santa shape."

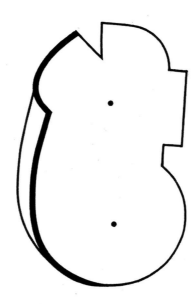

This pattern has been reshaped to create a slight bust-line for a young lady bear. The waist is slightly narrower than the basic pattern. This is referred to as the "teen girl" pattern.

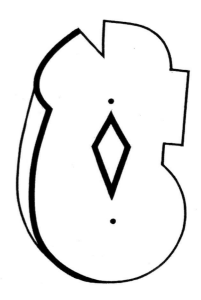

This version of the lady bear pattern has had a waist dart added to narrow the waist even more. This is referred to as the "fashion lady" pattern.

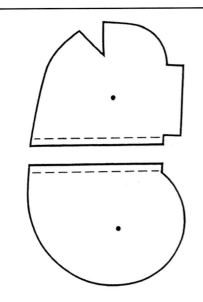

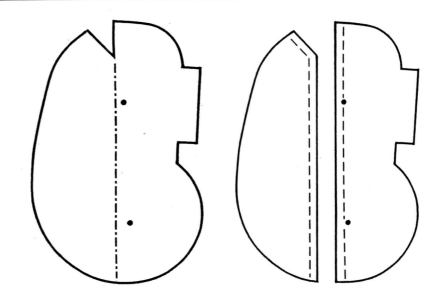

TWO-TONE
TWO-PART BODY

Two-tone bears offer a unique and charming aspect to any Teddy Bear creation.

Pandas, as well as many other bears, can be rendered in two tones. A bear might have a tan face and tummy set into a dark brown head and body. Maybe the inside of his ears are a lighter shade too. Some artists use a matching lighter color fur on the foot and paw pads to complete the effect.

To create a two-color body you must first design the body profile that you want. Depending on the design, you must split the body pattern into two parts from side to side or top to bottom. After you split the pattern you must add a quarter-inch seam allowance to the two pattern halves.

When creating a front-to-back two-part, two-color body pattern you must first draw a center line from the center point of the top V-cut dart to the center of the body bottom. Make certain that the line falls in front of the arm and leg joint holes. Split the pattern in half and add a quarter-inch seam allowance to each side of the pattern.

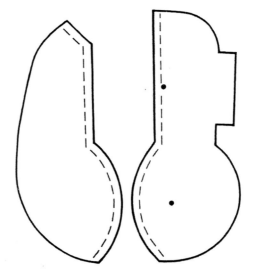

To create a four-piece body design where you might want to add more fullness to either the top or bottom of the body pattern, just draw a center line from top to bottom as described in the panel above.

Then change the shape as you want, add the quarter-inch seam allowance and you have a new, more fully shaped, body.

REDESIGNING THE ARM PATTERN

The arm pattern can be easily redesigned by a system of cut-and-move actions. First cut a line from the inside of the arm to the sewing line by the elbow. You can also cut a similar line at the wrist where the paw pad joins the arm.

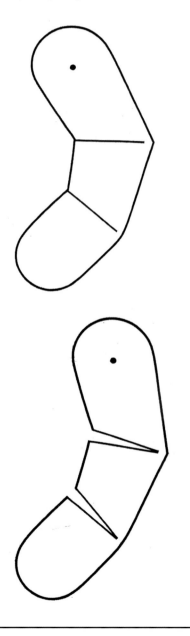

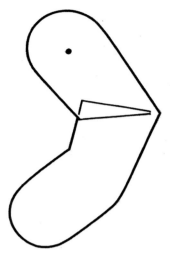

To bend the arm upward, just move the pieces into the new position and tape together. You can do the same thing for the wrist.

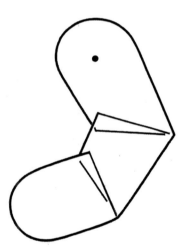

One note of caution: Do not bend the arm too tightly together. After you sew and stuff the arm it will tighten up and look even more bent. The best approach is to design the pattern slightly less bent than you finally want.

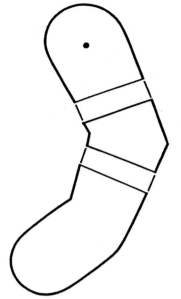

To straighten the arm a bit more than the basic pattern, just move the lower portion into the position you want, fill in the gap, and tape together.

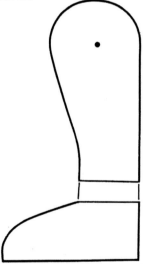

To add length to the arm, just insert extra pattern paper at two sections above and below the elbow.

To add length to the leg, just insert extra pattern paper at the ankle.

There are a number of ways to create a neck for your bear. One very simple way is to reduce the size of the disk inside the head which leaves you more room for stuffing. Leave the larger disk inside the body to create a shoulder. (see illustration below)

The diagrams at the right illustrates how a neck is added to the body pattern. You must determine how wide the neck must be to accommodate the disk and you must add a flap to cover the disk.

Or, you can add a neck to your head patterns by inserting a length of pattern paper between the head and the base covering piece. Be sure that you add equal length pieces to all three patterns—both profiles and the back end of the gusset.

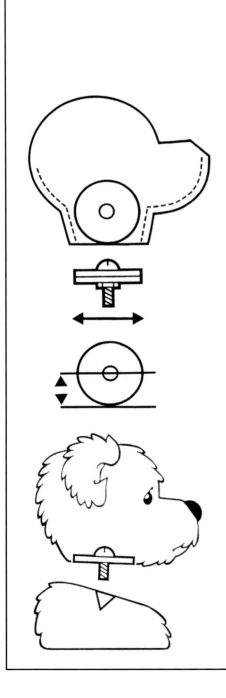

Working with the basic patterns you can alter the attitude of your bear's head by changing the location of the dart hole at the top of the body pattern. The further forward you move the hole the more your bear will look downward. The more you move it back the bear's head will tilt upward.

Another way to change the tilt of your bear's head is to alter the shape of the disk covering flap at the base of the head profile. To make the bear's head tilt downward just add some length to the back of the patterns. Be sure to add an equal amount to the back of the center gusset.

To create an upward tilt to your bear's head just add some length to the front of the neck. In this case the change only applies to the two profile pieces because the length of the back of the pattern remains the same so the center gusset is not involved.

CREATING GIRLS AND BOYS

Many Teddy Bear designers struggle with the age-old problem of the sexes. No, not the one about getting a date for the Saturday night dance, but the far more complex issue of how to make a bear look either feminine or masculine.

Looking at the general characteristics of boys and girls, we note that boys have bigger shoulders and narrower hips. Girls have softer shoulders and far more voluptuous hips. By changing the size of the joints you use, and without changing your basic pattern, you can create a more feminine or masculine looking bear.

But first let's look at what happens when you change the disk size in a joint. By a direct ratio, the smaller the disk the more room you have for stuffing and the heavier the look. Using a larger disk reduces the available area to add stuffing, so the result is slimmer.

Looking at the two bears above, the one on the left has softer shoulders and fuller hips, indicating a definite feminine nature. The bear on the right has broader shoulders and flatter hips which gives him a more manly stance. By changing the size of the disks you change the shape of the tops of the arms and legs and, therefore, the gender of the bear.

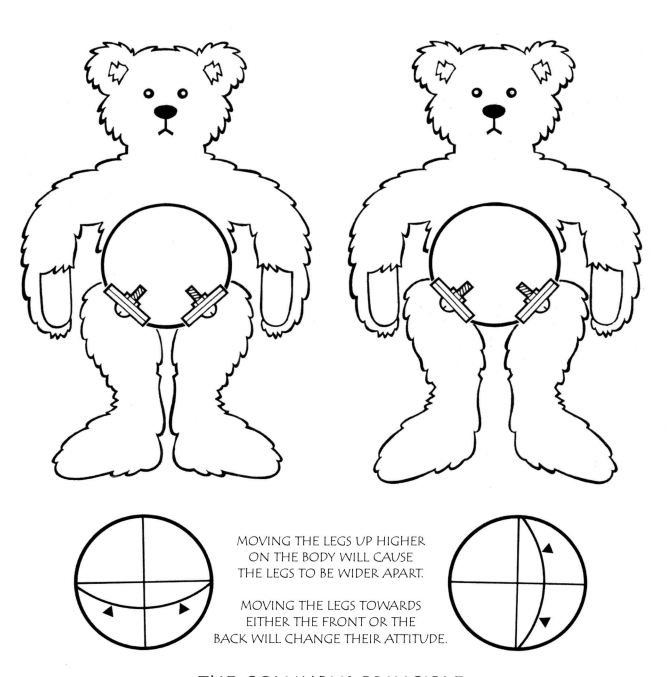

MOVING THE LEGS UP HIGHER
ON THE BODY WILL CAUSE
THE LEGS TO BE WIDER APART.

MOVING THE LEGS TOWARDS
EITHER THE FRONT OR THE
BACK WILL CHANGE THEIR ATTITUDE.

THE COLUMBUS PRINCIPLE

History tells us that Columbus discovered America by accident, which doesn't surprise me in the least. Travelling around a globe is no easy task, especially if everyone thinks it is flat instead of round. This also applies to the transition from flat pattern to the rounded out, stuffed version of your bear. Brilliant engineering aside, here is the Columbus principle in action when it comes to placing arms and legs on your bear's body.

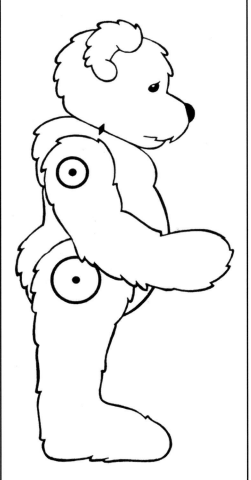

TRICKS WITH JOINTS

Changing the disk size can alter the gender of your Teddy Bear. However, changing the position of the disk inside both the body and the arms and legs changes your Teddy Bear's stance and attitude. In fact, it can change his entire personality.

As you look at the basic pattern you will see that in every place where there is a joint disk indicated there are three holes. The black dot hole in the middle, marked A, indicates the normal, standard position for the positioning hole in the body or the arms and legs. One either side of the black dot are two open circles marked B and C. These indicate either forward or backward positioning.

DUCKY BEAR

To create a duck-footed bear with welcoming arms simply select the disk hole marked C on the body, arm, and leg patterns. Use this hole to mark your fabric. By moving the arms and legs back they will turn outward. This will be further enhanced by moving them back on the body as well. Once again this is the Columbus Principle at work.

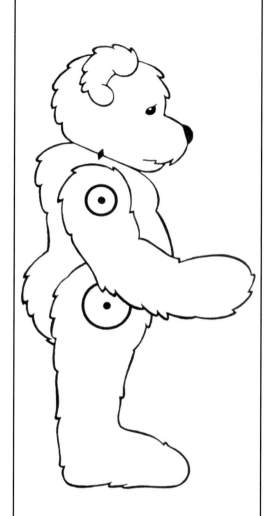

PIGEON BEAR

To create a pigeon-toed bear with turned-back arms simply select the disk hole marked B on your the body, arm, and leg patterns. Use this hole to mark your fabric. By moving the arms and legs forward they will turn inward. This will be further enhanced by moving them back on the body as well. Once again this is the Columbus Principle at work.

In the illustration at the far left we see a bear with his arms spread open in a welcoming gesture. His feet are spread apart in what might be called a duck-footed position. Or, if you prefer, a ballet-type position. These positions are achieved by simply moving the disk hole in the body and the arms and legs.

In the illustration above we see a bear with his arms turned inward and his feet turned inward as well. His feet appear to be pigeon-toed and his one arm seems to be behind his back while the other appears to be posed forward and inward. This is achieved by simply moving the disk hole forward in the body and in the arms and legs.

LEND AN EAR

Ok, listen up, this is all about ears. Many Teddy Bear artists think that ears are the most important element that gives character to their bears in a way that the eyes, nose, and mouth do not.

There are many types of ears but when all is said and done, they really fall into three styles with two different ways to attach them to the bear's head.

You can sew them on after the head is stuffed or you can sew them into the head before you stuff it. I prefer the latter method because it avoids hand-sewing and it is stronger and more uniform.

There is nothing more difficult than trying to line up the ears evenly on a finished head.

Now, I'll explain how to use ears to express your bear's mood or personality.

The three types of ears are: BASIC, PERKY, and PUPPY.

The BASIC ear has a straight bottom edge.

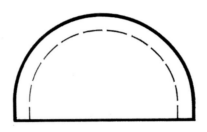

The BASIC ear is usually just flat and has little or no shape but it can be given some shape with a dart sewn on the inside piece of the ear.

Also the BASIC ear is the one used when you are sewing it on after the head is stuffed.

You can curve and shape it when you pin it into position.

The PERKY ear stands up and makes the bear look alert.

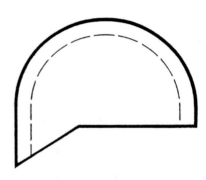

An ear that is PERKY has an extended corner on one side.

The PUPPY ear makes the bear look more somber and subdued because it lays flatter—like a scolded puppy.

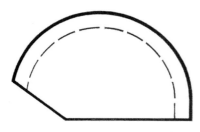

And a PUPPY ear has a clipped corner on one side.

The PUPPY and PERKY ears get shaped automatically when they are sewn into the head before stuffing.

Trace your ear pattern making two right and two left sides. I always draw the sewing line as well so that I have a perfect curve to my ears.

Cut them out and pin together making sure the fur tucks inside the ear. Sew the curved edge making sure to back-stitch the end to secure the stitches.

Always comb out the fur from the seam both inside and out. Then either clip the seam allowance so that it will curve easily or reduce the seam allowance by one-eighth of an inch.

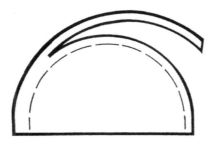

Use a blunt tool to push out the top curve of the ear so that it is well shaped.

To close the bottom of the ear just use a tiny bit of fabric glue along the edge—just enough to hold it in place.

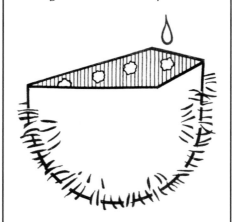

Or, you can do a quick whip-stitch along the edge.

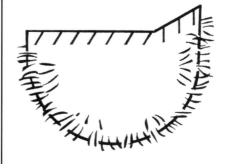

TEDDY TIP

If the ear is going to be sewn on after the head is stuffed, you must sew the ears a bit differently. In order to have a nice finished edge after you turn out the ear you must sew a part of the bottom edge as well. Start at point A and sew around the end tip, up over the top curve, around the other end tip and stop at point B. Turn out to the fur side and you will see that the ends are nicely finished.

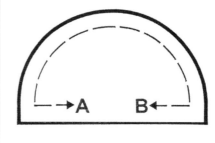

A SIMPLE FOUR-PIECE HEAD PATTERN

This head design is an original innovation based, in part, on a doll making trick I learned years ago. Adapting it to Teddy Bears was inspired by the need to create a set of simple patterns for a one-day workshop.

This simple ear design can also be used with the regular three-piece head.

A pattern for that design is included with the other three-piece head profile patterns.

This is a variation on the traditional center-seam head.

After you stuff the head you'll see that it takes on the look of a regular three-piece head even without a gusset.

This pattern is not easily modified without a certain amount of trial and error but it could be worth it if you are looking for a way to make a quick-n-easy Teddy Bear.

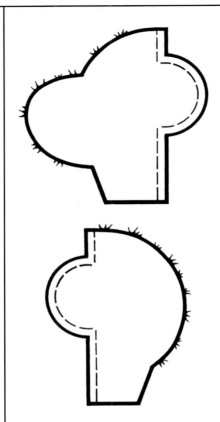

Begin by laying out, tracing, and cutting the four pieces—one left and right of each. I usually also trace the sewing line for the ear as well to insure sewing an even curve.

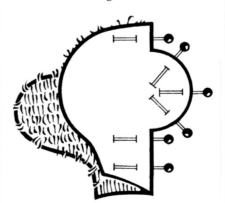

Next pin the front and back pieces together, fur side to fur side, making sure you push all the fur inside the head.

Then sew the front and back pieces together from top to bottom. Comb all of the fur out of the seam both front (fur side) and back.

Cut the seam allowance down to one-half the size, about one-eighth of an inch.

Turn the ear right side out, make sure it is completely turned out and shaped into a smooth curve, then comb the fur until it is fluffy.

Next, with the nose side up, comb a part in the fur from the top of the ear (B) to the bottom (A).

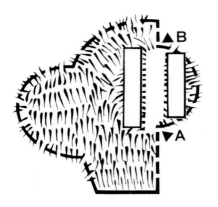

After you have made a perfect part in the fur you can tape it back with transparent tape.

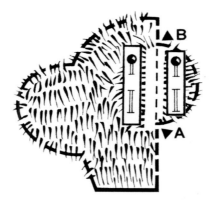

Pin the tape to the fabric to hold it in place. This will make sewing the seam easier.

Starting at the bottom of the ear (A to B) sew a seam to close the two halves of the ear together.

I suggest that you turn and resew the seam a second time to make sure it is secure.

Comb out the back of the seam where the stitching caught fur behind the ear.

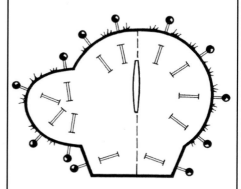

Now, pin the two sides of the head together, fur side to fur side.

Make sure the fur is all tucked inside the head.

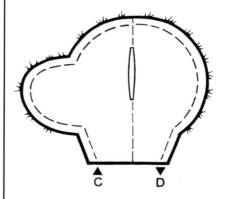

Sew the center seam starting in front under the chin and ending at the back of the neck. (C to D)

Comb out the seams inside and out.

That's it!

A TeddyBear may be purchased; but his love is without price.

UNDERSTANDING FUR

There are many different fur materials available today and they all make wonderful Teddy Bears and other stuffed critters. Many artists work with real, recycled fur from old coats or blankets. Others use inexpensive synthetic fur available from their local craft or fabric shop. The choice of fabric is a personal one and each type has advantages and disadvantages.

I work exclusively in mohair. Mohair is made from goat hair and is generally imported from either Germany or England. There are a few other countries that manufacture mohair but their goods are not as readily available. There are a number of subtle differences between English and German mohair but they do not drastically affect the final creation. Generally speaking, the most significant difference is the backing. German backing is tighter and a bit more regular in its weave. Probably only an experienced bear artist would notice the difference, and there are enough variations to confuse even the keenest eye. Just as most of us have a favorite brand of coffee, my personal fur preference is German mohair. Just one of the many how-you-might choices you can make.

All mohair comes in a vast array of styles, lengths, and colors. It also comes in a range of density from sparse to extra dense. Artists working to achieve the look of an old worn bear might select a sparse mohair while another artist might choose a dense fur for a more luxurious, cuddly look and feel. The choice of fur is the first step towards creating your own unique Teddy Bear. Usually we don't choose fur until after the bear has been envisioned and translated into a final pattern. But there are artists who begin with the fur choice just as there are dress designers who are inspired by the look and feel of a specific fabric.

One specific advantage to using mohair is that it is a natural fiber, and that means it can be styled just as any natural hair can be. If you want to straighten out certain sections of a curly fur, you can. And you can use many of the same products and techniques a hairdresser might use when styling your hair.

WORKING WITH MOHAIR

Someone always asks what sort of animal a "Mo" is. Wisecracks aside, mohair is actually made from goat hair and is processed in much the same way that sheep's wool is.

Of course, because it is a natural fiber, mohair can be colored and curled a number of ways. And, because it is a natural fiber, it can be restyled with most hair products.

The best type of comb to use on mohair is the kind used for pets because they have smooth metal teeth that won't cut the mohair the way plastic combs do.

Cutting mohair is an art all by itself and requires some practice and skill. You must only cut the backing, never the fur itself.

I tell my students that they should be able to cut out a bear without one single hair falling to the ground.

A really expert cutter can do that!

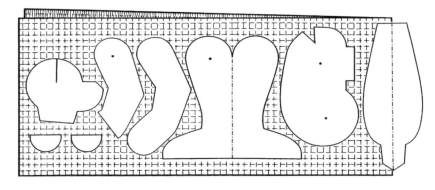

When you lay out patterns you should keep the pieces interlocking as tightly as possible to avoid waste. If you don't have a full set of patterns (most people don't make two sets of everything) and you want to determine if your piece of fabric is large enough, just fold it in half, lay the gusset pattern on the center line, and then lay out the single set of patterns. If they fit, you have enough.

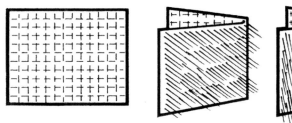

If you have any doubt as to what the direction of the fur is just fold one edge (top to bottom) and see how the fur lays. Then fold the fabric in the other direction (side to side) to see which looks better.

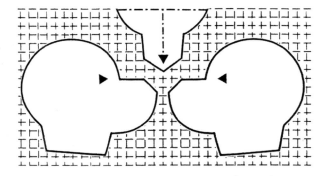

Your absolute guide is the weave of the fabric backing, not the fur itself. Always follow the vertical and horizontal threads as your guides. Line up the top edge of the nose on the same horizontal thread line so that your nose hair will be even on both sides. Line up the vertical center-line of the gusset on a vertical thread line so that both sides of the gusset will be even.

NUTS AND BOLTS

The process of jointing a bear can be a complicated one but fortunately there is a system that makes it a lot easier.

Basically, all jointing works on the same principle, two disks held together as a joint.

The original Teddy Bears were jointed this way and the joints were held together with a cotter pin.

Many artists still use this technique but it doesn't give you tight joints.

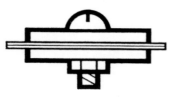

The system I use is based on two pressed-wood joints held together with a steel bolt and a lock-nut. Lock-nuts have a nylon lining in the thread area so that when you screw it on to the bolt the threads cut into the nylon liner and "lock" into place.

To make things even easier, I use 5-Minute Epoxy to glue the bolt into one disk.

This allows you to insert that bolt into the head, arms, and legs when you're stuffing them.

You can completely finish the head with the joint inside, gather the neck allowance around the disk and sew it closed.

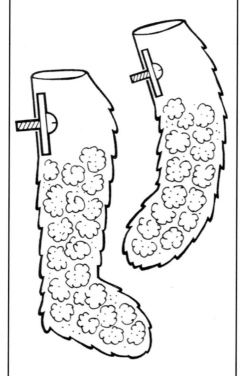

You can stuff and close the tops of the arms and legs with the joint already inside.

All this allows you to finish all the parts before you assemble them into the body and finish stuffing.

Because the bolt is glued into place you can screw the nut on without having to hold the bolt in place.

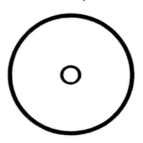

TEDDY TIP

When assembling the head, arms, and legs on the body it is best to do the legs first, then the head, and then the arms.

I have found this to be the best sequence, and one that allows you the easiest access to the joints and bolts with your nut turner.

41

A STITCH IN TIME

After you lay out your design, and carefully cut the pieces, you are ready to begin the sewing process. There are a few steps to take before you begin. First trim away the fur in the indicated areas.

Then, use Fray-Check to seal the open edges. There are artists who trim away all the fur from the seam allowance and Fray-Check every edge, but they probably carry an umbrella 24 hours a day as well.

Sewing ears on is a more or less traditional technique, but I find it difficult and very time consuming so I've come up with a fairly easy way to sew them into the head prior to stuffing.

All commercially-made bears have sewn-in ears, so it can't be a bad thing to learn.

Sewing the head is, of course, a more complex process and I have tried almost every method imaginable. About the only absolute rule I can stress is careful pinning, or basting, wins the day.

You can free-sew (no pins) many parts of a bear but not the head or the foot pads. These two items require a great deal of caution and precision if you want them to come out perfectly.

There are three areas where I always draw a sewing line on my fabric pieces.

First, the nose tip because I want to be certain that I get an even-sided tip.

Second, the paw pads because, again, I want a nice curve to the tip of the paw.

And, last, the foot pads because nothing shows sloppy sewing more than uneven foot pads.

Personally, I pin all my pieces before sewing them. It takes much more time to pin than it does to sew, but I feel it's worth it because I always have perfectly matched pieces when I'm finished and that's a good start towards making a beautifully crafted Teddy Bear.

PREPARING THE FABRICS

Begin by laying out your pattern pieces on the back of your fur. I always steam press the fur backing to iron out any wrinkles. I also discovered that the steam reactivates the sizing and tends to slightly stiffen up the backing.

I also use iron-on interfacing on the back of the felt or ultra suede that will be used for the paw and foot pads.

This will reduce the stretch of these fabrics and is a good surface to draw on.

Always use a permanent marking pen to outline your patterns.

Cut out all of the pieces, being careful to cut only the backing and not the fur.

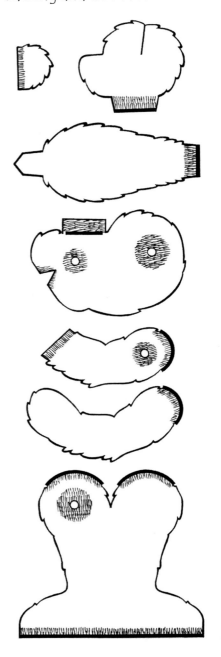

Trim away the fur in the areas indicated by the shaded area on this diagram.

Finally, Fray-Check all the edges where there is a heavy black line in the diagram.

SEWING IN THE EARS

This is an easy process if you follow the instructions carefully. First I'll describe how to sew in the BASIC ear because that is the easiest, and uses only the first step of the process.

You should have two finished ears with the bottom edge glued or sewn closed. The bottom edge should have a quarter-inch of the fur trimmed away. The slash in the head should also have a quarter-inch of fur trimmed away as well.

First, glue, or pin, one side of the ear opening to the ear and make sure you are one-quarter inch below the top of the head. (A)

Next, glue, or pin, the other half of the ear opening to the other side of the ear. (B)

Then, sew the ear into the head and be sure to finish off at the center dot. (C)

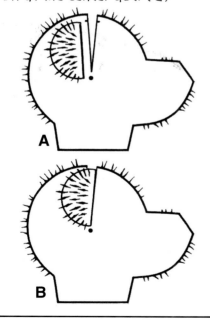

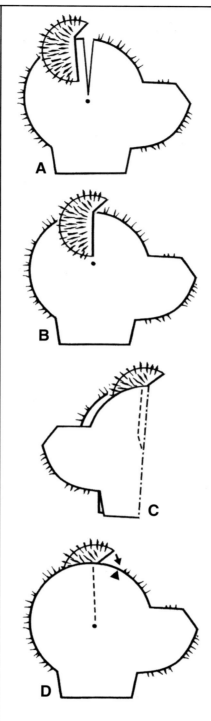

If you are using a PUPPY or PERKY ear you must cut a notch in the ear, then fold it forward and glue, or stitch, it to the edge of the head. (D)

SEWING THE GUSSET

This can be a bit tricky but not all that difficult. Note that I have designed the tip of the nose with hard angles. This is to make aligning and pinning easier.

This is also why I draw the tip of the nose on my gusset pattern because it doesn't follow the squared-off shape of the pattern.

Pin one side of the head profile to one side of the gusset, making sure the ear is tucked down inside so you don't get it caught in the sewn seam. Sew the gusset and profile together. Repeat the process for the other profile.

Then, line up the two profiles from the nose tip to the bottom of the neck and sew together. Make sure that all your seams come together as indicated by this diagram.

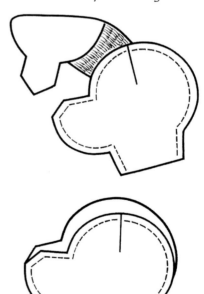

SEWING PAW PADS AND FOOT PADS

Sewing foot pads can be a nightmare and there is no easy way to do them. Over the years I have discovered that even the most skilled artists have trouble with foot pads.

The best way to get them sewn in as perfectly as possible is to use a sewing-line to follow when you are sewing.

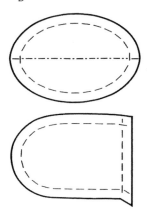

First, pin the pad into the foot and then whip-stitch or running-stitch it into place.

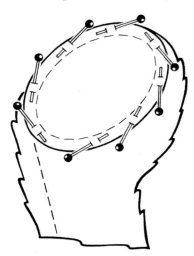

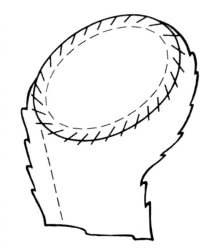

When the leg is in the sewing machine, foot pad up, you'll need a flat tool, like a butter knife, to push all of the leg material out of the way from under the pressure foot.

DON'T ever lift up the pressure foot until after you have finished sewing your first complete round of stitches.

If you did not sew it correctly the first time around just go back and re-stitch any of the parts you missed.

Attach the paw pad to the wrist section of the arm before you sew the two arm pieces together.

THE MAGIC FLAP

There is a flap of fabric on the back of the body where the stuffing opening is located. This gets folded back and glued down inside the body.

Glue only the outer edge, not the fold.

This folded flap helps when you are closing up the body. It is much stronger than just a quarter-inch of seam allowance.

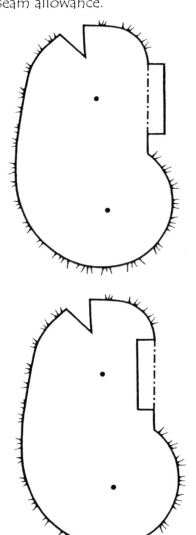

THE LADDER STITCH

The ladder stitch is the most important stitch in bearmaking and also the most difficult to learn and master. I suggest that you practice on scraps of fabric before you try it on your bear. This is your basic closing stitch and it is used to close the tops of the arms and legs as well as the back of the body.

Begin by taking a long piece of carpet or upholstery thread and making a large knot at the end. Poke the needle through the wrong side to the right side at the corner of one side of the opening you want to close. Now, working from side to side, keep thinking in-out, cross over, in-out, cross over.

Your stitches should be about 3/16" long with the same amount of space between stitches. You can tighten your stitches as you sew along the opening. Make sure that the fabric folds in and disappears inside the opening. When you have finished the stitches you can pull the thread tight and create a locking stitch at the end of the sewn line. Finally, bury the tail of your thread inside the stuffed part of your bear.

With your knot inside the opening, follow the numbers from 1 to 10. Keep in mind the little working thought: in-out, cross over, in-out, cross over...

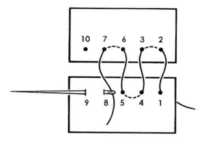

The fabric should turn under as you tighten your stitches but if they don't then just push them in with your needle or any pointed object.

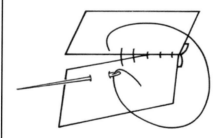

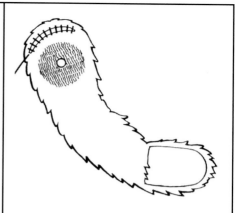

After you close the top of the arms and legs you can tie off your thread behind the disk.

Another good thing to do is trim back the fur from the disk area. This will allow you to have tighter joints.

Close the head by using a running stitch around the bottom of the neck flap. Gather the fabric around the base of the bolt and tie it off.

STUFF IT!

Teddy Bears have been stuffed with almost everything imaginable. The first bears were filled with straw-like excelsior. Bears have been stuffed with wood chips and birdseed as well as shredded dollar bills from the US Mint. In recent years there have been trends towards pellets made from sand and glass as well as metal shot. But, after all is said and done, I prefer a nice fluffy Poly-Fil that is clean and easy to work with.

For as many possible stuffing materials that exist, there are an equal number of potential stuffing tools.

Add to that the variety of choices for various degrees of softness or firmness and you have almost limitless ways to fill up your Teddy Bear.

I stuff my bears so hard that they feel as though they are made of cement. I don't think of my bears as toys to be cuddled but rather as pieces of fabric sculpture that usually are in a standing position, dressed in an outfit and ready to amuse and delight.

My jointing and stuffing system allows me to finish all of the arms and legs as well as the head before I joint them to the body. The last thing I stuff and close is the body.

Basically, I use a variety of stuffing tools that are either actual screw drivers or wooden versions of screw drivers. Usually, I tape the tip of real screw drivers to keep them from ripping the fabric. Recently I discovered a plastic product you can dip the tip into as a protective covering.

The real secret of firm stuffing is not power or strength but persistence and patience. I used to power stuff and work up a great sweat and lose a few pounds in the process, but then I realized that it was all a matter of air and pressure.

When you open a box or bag of Poly-fil it literally explodes into a giant mound of stuffing because they suck the air out when they pack it to keep the size minimal.

Working backwards produces the same effect. Now I just patiently tap the stuffing down inside the parts, forcing out the excess air until the piece is as firm as I want. It actually gets a little bit firmer after a day or so as the air escapes through the fabric and the stuffing expands even more.

There are a few tricks to help you get the desired effect of a well-stuffed bear.

THE HEAD

I finger stuff most of the head so that I can control the shape. I begin by putting in a small amount of stuffing in the nose. Then I fill most of the head with a fair amount of stuffing to see the shape. I continue to fill the head by pushing more and more stuffing into the center of the head, forcing the outer stuffing to expand. This technique avoids getting lumpy sections in the head. The last thing I stuff is the nose because if I do it sooner the stuffing will back up into the head. Once the head is fully stuffed it is easy to hard-stuff the nose until it is firm. It is very important to stuff the tip of the nose as firmly as possible so that you will have a firm surface to embroider over.

TEDDY TIP

One of the easiest ways to hard-stuff the tip of the nose or the tip of the toes is to push more stuffing into the nose, or toes, along the seam line.

THE ARMS

It is best to hard-stuff the end of the paw so that you get a nice rounded shape. Then stuff the rest of the arm to the degree of firmness you want.

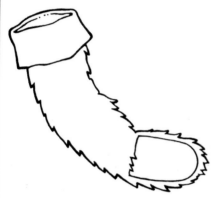

THE LEGS

Stuff the foot, especially the toe section, firmly. Then finish stuffing the leg to the desired firmness.

NOTE: If you intend to have your bear stand up, then at least hard- stuff the ankles as well as the foot.

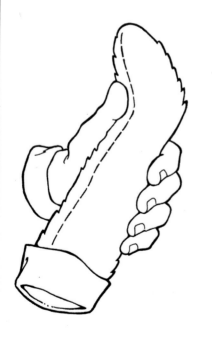

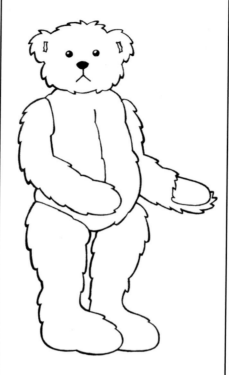

BEWARE of the Egyptian Virus that can cause your bear's arms and legs to both point in the same direction the way the figures do on Egyptian wall paintings. This is caused by the way you hold the arm or leg when you stuff it. If you are right-handed then most likely you hold the arm or foot in your left hand and stuff in the same direction for all four limbs. However, this will cause them to all face in the same direction, creating the Egyptian Virus effect. Hold the arm and leg with the paw and toe facing upward, and stuff them in a straight direction to avoid the twisted, Egyptian Virus effect.

THE BODY

This can be a bit tricky and requires a bit of restraint on the bear's part.

I tie the bear's ankles together so that the joints will be in the correct position and the bear will stand up correctly. I tie the wrists as well so that the shoulders will "pop" out and beeven.

Because I have used disks with glued-in bolts, I can stuff and close all my parts before final jointing.

This allows me to work on each individual piece, which is a lot more manageable.

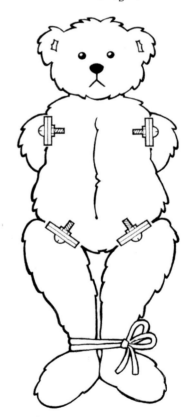

TeddyBear: price on the ticket; value in the heart.

LET'S FACE IT

There can be no question that the face is the most important aspect of the Teddy Bear. Beautiful clothing and accessories or even expert craftsmanship can not win out over a charming expression. There are Teddy Bear artists who have a distinctive head design that they repeat again and again, with slight variation, to the constant delight of their collectors. Other artists have an overall style, or look, that can be recognized in any bear they create. Both of these traits are reflected in every other field of art. For example, no matter the subject or style, we recognize a Picasso as easily as we can identify the distinctive style of Grandma Moses.

Creating a wonderful head and facial expression on your Teddy Bear can be a challenge and a joy. And the paths that artists use to reach that destination are as varied as the artists themselves. There are designers who insist that it is all in the basic pattern they create. And, in their case, it might be true. Others say their nose design is their trademark. And many say that everything depends on how they place the eyes into the face that marks their creation. In fact, they are all correct about themselves and their creations.

Many artists sew the bear's ears on last because they say it is the final touch that gives full expression to their bear. Others suggest the exact placement, or size, of the eyes is the secret; while many say it is in the expression of the mouth. Again, all of these are equally true of specific artists but they are not true of all artists. I enjoy a certain reputation for my nose design which clearly identifies my bears as much as my signature, but I place the eyes in last because I feel that creates the final touch that gives life to my Teddy Bear creation.

Once again we see that there are many ways you might approach an aspect of your bearmaking. If designing patterns, selecting fur, carefully stitching, and stuffing your bear is the meat and potatoes of bearmaking, creating the facial expression is definitely the dessert. Those last few moments of the creative process are what make all of the previous struggles worthwhile. Enjoy!

PERFECT NOSES EVERY TIME

When I first started to make bears I quickly realized that one aspect of the process that I did not enjoy at all was anything that required hand-sewing.

That's why I developed techniques to sew the ears in by machine instead of sewing them on by hand.

Another, more difficult, task was embroidering on the nose and mouth. After years of collecting Teddy Bears I knew that a poorly sewn nose could ruin the face of even the most expertly crafted bear.

After dozens of failed attempts, I created a technique that was almost foolproof, even for me.

My technique became almost a trademark of my bears and people would comment on my hand-sewing technique. If they only knew the truth!

Over the years, I have taught hundreds of bearmakers these secrets and tricks so that they can enjoy the pleasure of sewing perfect noses every time.

This takes patience and practice but if you follow these step-by-step instructions you will soon develop an excellent technique that will impress even the most critical observer.

Prepare the nose tip of the gusset pattern by trimming and shaving the nose tip area that will be embroidered over. You should do this before you sew the head together.

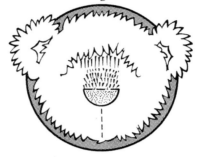

The next most important factor is in making sure that you stuff the head, especially the tip of the nose, very firmly. Even if you intend to make a cuddly, soft bear you should firm-stuff the head and really get the nose tip as hard as you possibly can.

A good trick is to color the nose tip area with a fabric permanent marker with a color similar to the color you are embroidering the nose.

Use a little bit of tacky glue-stick over this to seal the color and harden the surface.

NOTE: The symbol of the needle and thread only indicates the position of the needle. Obviously, the thread continues between stitches in all of the illustrations.

The best trick of all is to use a second very thin coat of tacky glue-stick over the surface as you embroider the nose. This helps to hold the embroidery thread in place.

Next, tape down the fur around the tip of the nose to keep it out of your way.

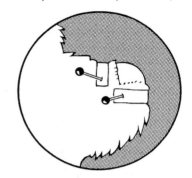

Pin the tape in place to hold it back tightly. Masking tape or mending tape work well for this process.

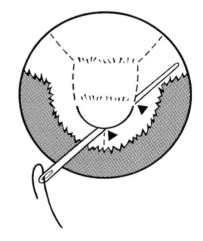

Now you can begin by inserting the needle into the very tip of the nose; holding the head with the nose facing away from you.

Start the embroidery by bringing the needle out at the top of the nose on the left side.

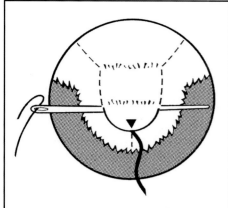

Leave about eight inches of thread hanging at the tip of the nose because this piece of thread will become your upper lip thread that holds the mouth in place.

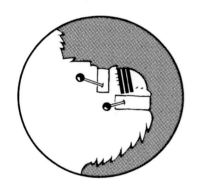

NOTE: Make sure that your needle always goes in and out just about an eighth-inch below the seam line. This is very important.

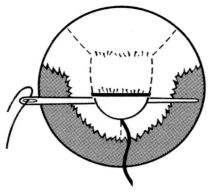

Then insert your needle into the head on the right side but do not push it through to the left side—yet. Next pull the thread across the bridge of the nose, behind the needle, and hold it in place with your finger.

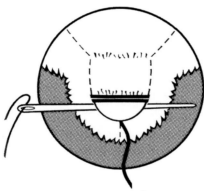

Next you push your needle through the head and come out one line below the previous stitch.

The term "one line" simply means one thread line of the fabric backing. Imagine a needlepoint grid and you get the picture.

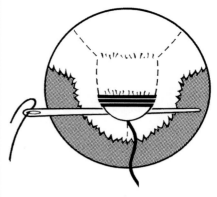

Very carefully repeat this process for each successive descending line of thread.

Make certain that the surface stays tacky from the glue-stick and add a little if the surface starts to dry out.

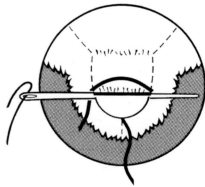

Remember the process: First insert your needle into the head on the right side but do not push it through to the left side—yet. Next pull your thread across the bridge of the nose, behind the needle, and hold it down in place with your finger.

I cannot emphasize this enough because when you have mastered this technique you will be able to embroider beautiful noses every time.

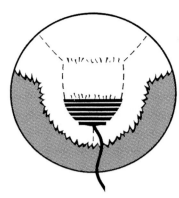

When you reach the tip of the nose, make the last stitch the same width as the previous one. This will help to avoid a too-pointed tip.

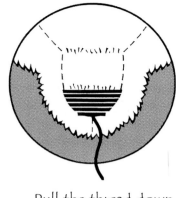

Pull the thread down along the side of the nose, under the dangling upper lip thread, and around to the right side of the nose.

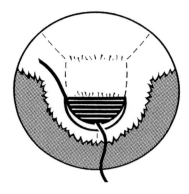

This is the nose shaping thread and you can pull it tight to bump up your nose a bit.

The second loop thread is your finishing thread and it completes the nose outline.

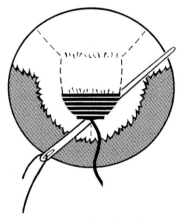

Now, with that last stitch, bring your needle back out at the top of the nose to the point where you began.

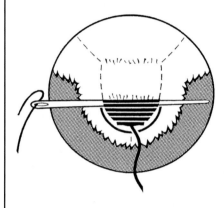

Insert the needle into the head and out on the left side just under the first looping thread.

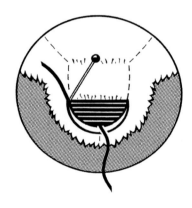

After you have reached the right side of the nose with the finishing thread just pin it down in place while you design the bear's mouth.

CREATING A MOUTH

This is a very simple process and a great deal of fun. Take three straight pins and place one at the bottom of the upper lip where you want it to end. Next, take a short length of embroidery thread, loop it over the pin, and play around with different positions and lengths for the mouth design.

When you have decided how long and wide apart the mouth lines will be, mark them with the other two pins.

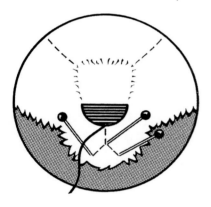

Now, take a long needle, thread the upper lip thread through it, and push it through the head coming out the back as close to the head disk as possible. Leave the loop loose in the front so that you can pass the mouth thread under it.

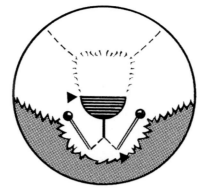

Then take the needle with the nose finishing thread and insert it just under the shaping thread. Push through the head and come out by the pin on the left side of the mouth.

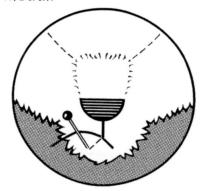

Loop that thread under the upper-lip thread, pull the upper-lip thread tight against the head, and then insert the needle where the third pin indicates the other side of the mouth.

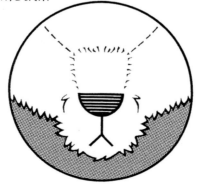

Again, push the needle out the back of the head.

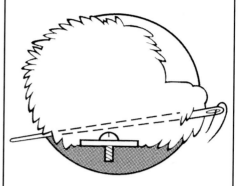

Bring your embroidery threads out of the back of the head, under the fur fabric and over the head disk.

Anchor them with a knot to prevent them from being pulled out when you are combing the bear's face.

Now you are ready to addthe eyes and groom the face.

THE EYES HAVE IT

It's been said that the eyes are the windows to the soul. I don't know if Teddy Bears have a soul, but they certainly do have a heart.

When it comes to selecting and placing eyes in your bear there are a number of choices and considerations.

Eyes come in a variety of styles: from shoe-button, to colored with black pupils, to black plastic or glass.

There are plastic safety eyes for use in children's bears.

And there are blown glass eyes for the artist-made bears.

Originally, Teddy Bears had shoe-button eyes made from leather-covered buttons created for the high-button shoes of 1903. These are still popular among certain artists who prize them for their romantic past and their hard-to-find quality.

I prefer the standard glass eyes on a wire loop that resemble shoe-button eyes but have more depth of color and sparkle.

When you reach the point of deciding what eyes your bear should have there are a number of things to consider.

A small point of interest is the fact that the human eye is the only organ in the body that never changes size. The eyes we are born with are the same size as the ones we die with.

That's why babies seem to have big eyes while old folks, whose lids have all wrinkled, seem to have smaller ones.

That's one way you can show age in a bear. Big eyes for youngsters and smaller ones for older bears.

Another consideration is gender. A girl bear looks more feminine with slightly larger eyes than the eyes used in a similar-size boy bear. That's because we usually see women wearing eye makeup, which creates the look of larger eyes.

Big eyes make the bear look brighter while small eyes make him look a bit dopey.

Take a look at cartoon characters and you will see that the cute, bright-eyed characters have large, wide-spaced eyes while the dopey characters have smaller, close-set eyes.

Selecting the style and color of your bear's eyes is the final touch that will give personality and character to your design. I always enjoy this last step of creation the most. It is a fairly simple process and one that brings a

great deal of satisfaction and delight. When the eyes are finally set, it is like the bear waking up and saying hello for the first time.

Safety eyes come in a variety of styles and usually have their own instructions, so I'll just describe the technique for setting in shoe-button style glass eyes.

These eyes come on a wire loop, but before you do anything else you must match up a pair of eyes making sure they are the same depth and diameter.

Take a 24-inch strand of carpet or upholstery thread and tie a knot in the loop with the thread. Make sure your two strands are equal length.

Then carefully, and gently, pinch the loop closed with your pliers.

Next put a slight bend in the wire stem.

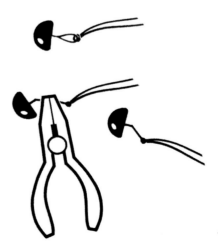

Mark the position of the eyes with black glass-head pins or even with black hat pins. Use anything that will approximate the eyes and allow you to play around with positioning and placement.

After you have decided where they eyes will go, take a thick, five-inch needle and push through the head at a diagonal angle so that the tip comes out under the bear's chin right at the curve of the neck.

The left eye thread should come out on the right side of the center seam of the bear's neck.

The right eye thread should come out on the left side of the center seam of the bear's neck.

With the bent section of the eye wire pointing downward, pull the eye into the head.

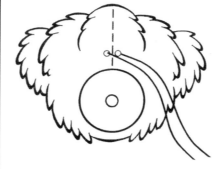

Then, using a surgeon's three-turn knot, tie the eyes tightly in position.

Tie a final locking knot and then place the tip of your needle into one of the holes the thread came through.

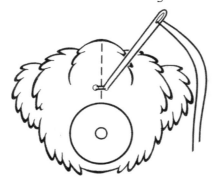

Thread the needle with all of the eye threads and pull the threads through the back of the head. Pull hard enough so that the knot will "pop" inside the head and disappear.

Clip off the thread ends and say hello to your Teddy.

SMALL, MEDIUM, AND LARGE

One of the greatest joys in bearmaking is the designing and styling of faces.

After all the problem solving of pattern making is over, and after all the pinning, and sewing, and stuffing is completed, all that remains is the face.

There are as many different Teddy Bear faces as there are people on the planet, and you can take one basic head pattern and change it into dozens of characters by a simple process of SMALL, MEDIUM, and LARGE.

That applies to the length of fur you choose, and to its density and style. The fur can be straight, or wavy, or curly, or tipped with two tones of color.

Then you can embroider the nose in a variety of colors and even change the size and shape with the number of stitches you use.

Finally, you can change the bear's entire expression by the size of eyes you use.

Just take a look at these different faces that are all drawn on the same basic head and you get the idea. Have fun!

FINAL TOUCHES

After all the tasks of cutting, sewing, stuffing, and closing are finished, and you have embroidered the nose and set the eyes, there remains only one final step to be taken to finish your bear. That final step is grooming the face.

There are a number of different ways to accomplish this final task. For instance, I know that my bear will have a trimmed nose bridge so I rough trim that part of the gusset before I sew the head together. I know that I will trim the fur behind the eyes so I usually do that at the same time as I do the nose bridge.

I know that no matter the style of the fur, I will want to straighten the fur on both sides of the nose. I also do part of this before I sew the head together.

But now the moment of truth has arrived and I'm ready to do those final steps to finish my bear's face.

First I carefully trim the bridge of the nose to the desired length. Some artists trim this area right down to the fabric backing. Others prefer to leave it long. I choose to modify the length so that I can clearly see the eyes.

To accomplish this I cut the fur in a rounded shape with the center being the crest of the curve.

Next, I hold down the fur above the upside-down V shape of the mouth and, using very sharp embroidery scissors, I cut the fur along that line.

Then, using barber's "thinning" scissors, I shape the fur around the mouth and reduce the length under the chin.

NOTE: The fur under the chin of the bear is visually the longest on his head because it is hanging straight down its full length. I always trim this back so that it looks the same as the side hair and retains the "look" of my original design.

TEDDY TIP

Because mohair is a natural fiber, you can "style" it the same way you do human hair. Plain water and some strong brushing will straighten most mohair but if you want to straighten curly or wavy hair you'll need more help. I use any non-alcohol based styling gel such as Dippity-Do or any of the other brands of spray-on, alcohol-free, styling gels.

This is NOT hair spray which contains both alcohol and lacquer.

Style is what you have, not what you wear.

WHEN A BOW IS NOT ENOUGH

If clothes make the man, what makes the Teddy Bear? Well, every Teddy loves a colorful bow—at least that is the case with the Teddys I've known. Many bears enjoy hats, scarves, lace collars, or a brightly colored sweater, as well as a smart vest or a charming pinafore.

Just as little girls enjoy dressing up in mommy's flowered hat and high-heel shoes, and little boys put on dad's fedora and topcoat to act grown up, Teddys enjoy the pretending that comes with a costume.

The most important thing to remember about clothing for the Teddy Bear, male or female, is that the outfit is intended to enhance, not obscure, the bear's own special quality. Costumes should maximize, not minimize, the beauty of the bear's fur and natural charm.

Teddy Bears do a lot of sitting around on beds and in chairs, so when selecting an outfit be sure that it will look attractive when the bear is sitting down. Teddy Bears tend to have short legs and long bodies with a bit of a tummy, so you must choose, or create, costumes that either enhance or disguise these features. Overalls and rompers are especially good for this purpose.

Teddys also like props such as eyeglasses, baskets of flowers, fun shoes, and a wide assortment of things that once belonged to children or dolls.

Over the years I've developed a number of clothing patterns that are as easy to use as the bear patterns themselves. And, they are every bit as versatile and open to interpretation. Once again, the basic patterns suggest how-you-might create a dress or vest pattern that will be uniquely your own and enhance the look of the special bear that you have created.

Clothing and accessories help to give your Teddy Bear personality and become a part of their story. And if there is one thing I know it is that every Teddy has a tale. But not every Teddy has a tail.

THE WELL-DRESSED TEDDY BEAR

Dressing a bear can be a lot of fun but it should not be a lot of work. Over the years I have developed some quick and easy patterns to create clever outfits for Adam and Eve.

Once again, the pattern pieces are easy to customize to your own style. One thing I have observed is that an overdressed Teddy distracts from the beauty of the bear itself. For that reason I have kept my designs basic and fairly understated.

The idea is to enhance the beauty of the bear while expressing his personality in an outfit.

The French designer, Coco Chanel, is quoted as saying that the true definition of chic is expressed by what a designer has left off. In other words, less is more and basic is beautiful.

So, with that in mind, here are some basic designs for rompers, pinafores, and garden gowns for Eve and some vests, jackets, and coveralls for Adam.

ALTERING BASIC CLOTHING PATTERNS

Once again all of the patterns can be altered by changing their outline or by cutting the pattern to enlarge or reduce it in size.

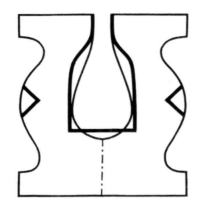

The bodice pattern can easily be changed to have a different neckline or a different cap-sleeve shape.

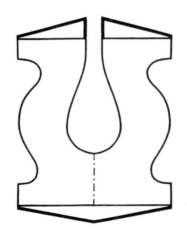

The bottom line of the bodice can be changed as well to create a more dramatic skirt treatment.

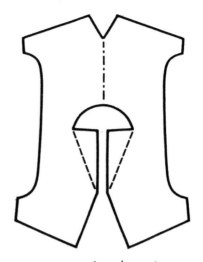

Vests can be altered to have a collar or changed into a jacket with sleeves.

Pockets can be added to pinafores, jackets, overalls, and vests to add detailing to the garment.

Vests and jackets can have a faux pocket by adding a simple pocket flap.

TEDDY TIP

When you make a basic bodice or vest, the easiest way to do it quickly is by lining the piece with organdy or another lightweight fabric.

I use just the sewing line pattern traced out on the lining fabric.

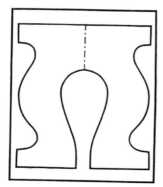

Then I pin that to my outer fabric. NOTE: Be sure to have the outer fabric right side up with the organdy over it.

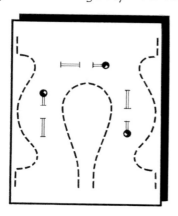

Just sew the sides and neckline, leaving the bottom of the front and back open so you can turn the piece right side out.

Cut away the seam allowance with pinking scissors before turning. Press flat with an iron.

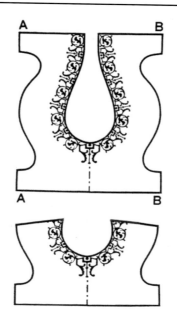

Then, after you have completed the bodice or vest, and added any trims, you can join the sides (A to A and B to B) and sew them together.

Always finish work on everything you add to the bodice before you close the sides.

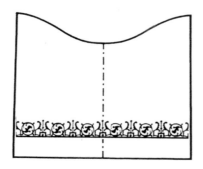

If you want to create an irregular hemline for your bear's ball-gown, it is easier to add trims and to sew the hem in a straight line. Instead of making the hemline irregular, you can make the top edge irregular instead.

The effect will be the same, but the work will be much easier.

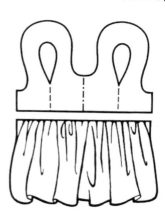

To attach the skirt to the bodice I find it easier to lay out the finished bodice and pin it flat so that the bottom edge is straight. Then, using a bit of fabric glue, attach the skirt to the bodice. Then sew the two pieces together. This is much quicker than pinning the pieces together and much easier to sew a straight line at the bottom of the bodice. This is especially true if you have shaped the bottom edge of the bodice.

DESIGNING SLEEVES

Most dressmakers will tell you that insetting a sleeve into a garment is a nightmare on wheels. If fact, that is true of clothing made for humans. But Teddy Bear outfits don't require the same degree of intricate fit and workmanship.

Since most bears have arms that just move from side-to-side, the design of sleeves is really quite easy. And, unlike the technique used for human garments, these sleeves are a snap to create, inset, and finish.

Like all of the patterns, the sleeve pattern can be made longer or shorter and even a bit wider for a giant puffed-sleeve effect.

You can simply gather the top edge of the sleeve or you can do folded tucks for a more tailored look.

I've even included some terrific tricks for making quick-and-easy pleats for sleeves and skirts.

And, like any of the patterns, the trims can be added easily before you sew the pieces together.

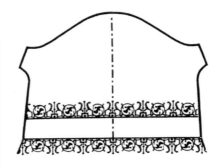

If you are adding trims to the sleeve, or lace along the bottom edge, it is easier to do it before you gather the sleeve.

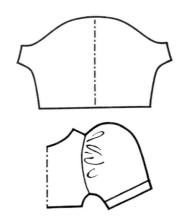

To create a short sleeve just use the standard sleeve with a finished edge. You can also make a cuff on this sleeve by adding some length to the pattern and then folding it up before you sew the sleeve closed.

To create a small puffed sleeve just use elastic in the edge of the standard pattern.

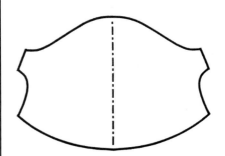

To create a larger puffed sleeve just add a bit of width to the sleeve pattern and curve the bottom edge.

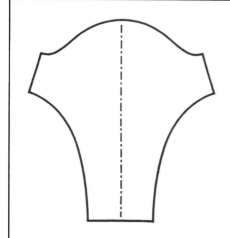

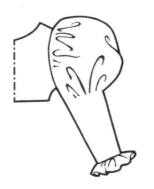

To create a version of a leg-o-mutton sleeve just design a longer version of the sleeve that tapers down to a tight lower sleeve.

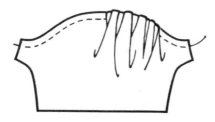

There are two ways to gather a sleeve. First, you can simply use a running stitch along the top edge or you can create a series of pleats and pin them in place before you sew.

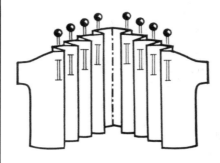

A quick-and-easy way to create even pleats is to make cardboard wedges that you form the pleats with. Just fold the fabric around the wedge and pin it in position.

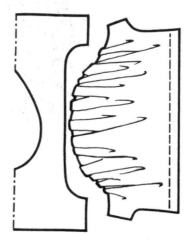

To inset the sleeve just pin or spot-glue it along the bodice sleeve opening edge. Then sew the sleeve in place.

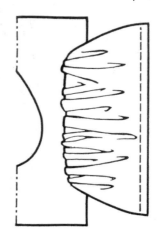

Fold over the bodice and sleeve, pin in position, and sew closed. I usually sew from the cuff edge back to the waist edge because the cuff edge is more critical to keep even.

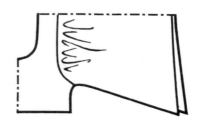

Dreams are the blueprints of reality.

A TeddyBear does not come to life until he is loved,
but once loved he will live forever.

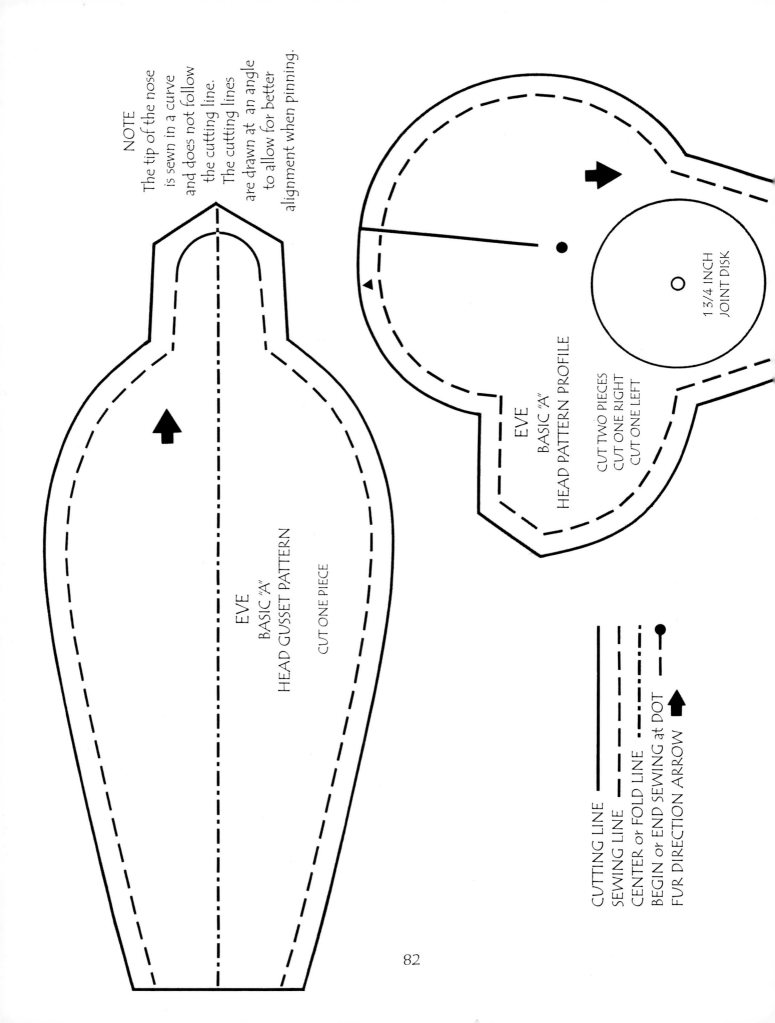

NOTE
The tip of the nose is sewn in a curve and does not follow the cutting line. The cutting lines are drawn at an angle to allow for better alignment when pinning.

EVE
BASIC "A"
HEAD GUSSET PATTERN

CUT ONE PIECE

EVE
BASIC "A"
HEAD PATTERN PROFILE

CUT TWO PIECES
CUT ONE RIGHT
CUT ONE LEFT

1 3/4 INCH
JOINT DISK

CUTTING LINE
SEWING LINE
CENTER or FOLD LINE
BEGIN or END SEWING at DOT
FUR DIRECTION ARROW

82

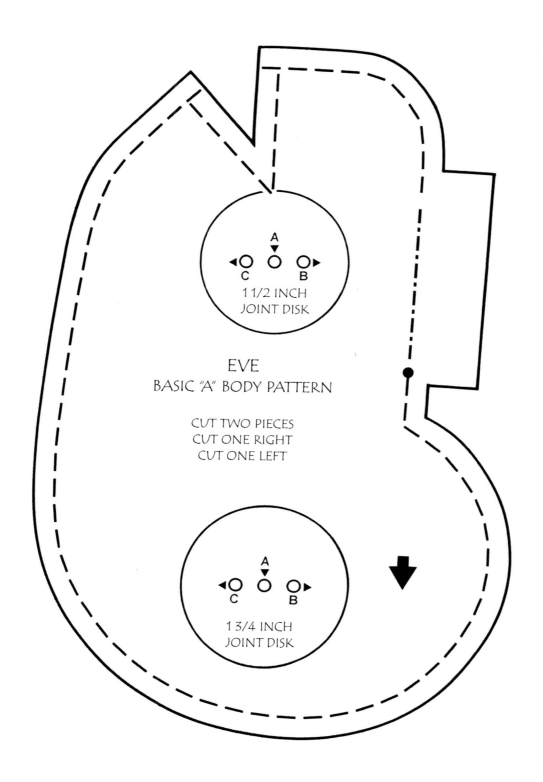

EVE
BASIC "A" BODY PATTERN

CUT TWO PIECES
CUT ONE RIGHT
CUT ONE LEFT

1 1/2 INCH
JOINT DISK

A
C   B

1 3/4 INCH
JOINT DISK

A
C   B

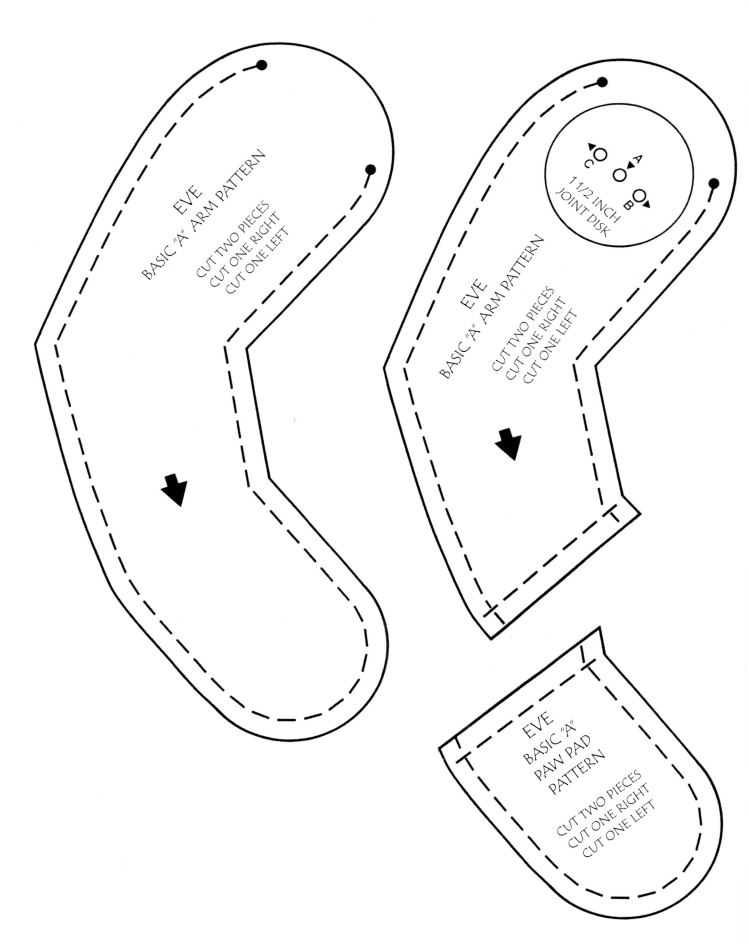

EVE
BASIC "A" ARM PATTERN

CUT TWO PIECES
CUT ONE RIGHT
CUT ONE LEFT

EVE
BASIC "A" ARM PATTERN

CUT TWO PIECES
CUT ONE RIGHT
CUT ONE LEFT

1 1/2 INCH
JOINT DISK

C
A
B

EVE
BASIC "A"
PAW PAD
PATTERN

CUT TWO PIECES
CUT ONE RIGHT
CUT ONE LEFT

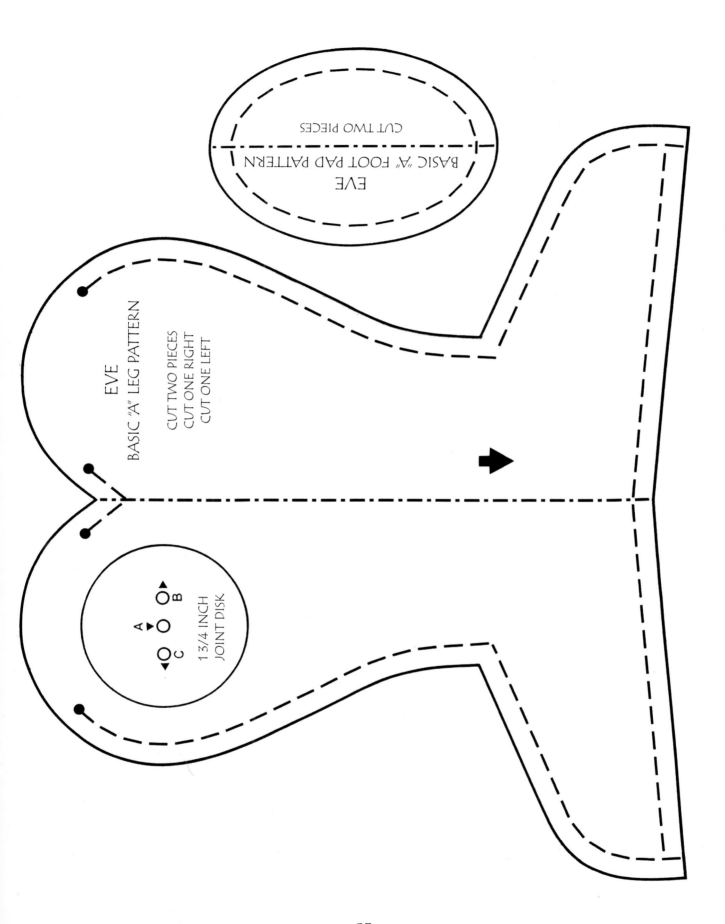

EVE
BASIC "A" FOOT PAD PATTERN
CUT TWO PIECES

EVE
BASIC "A" LEG PATTERN

CUT TWO PIECES
CUT ONE RIGHT
CUT ONE LEFT

A
B
C

1 3/4 INCH
JOINT DISK

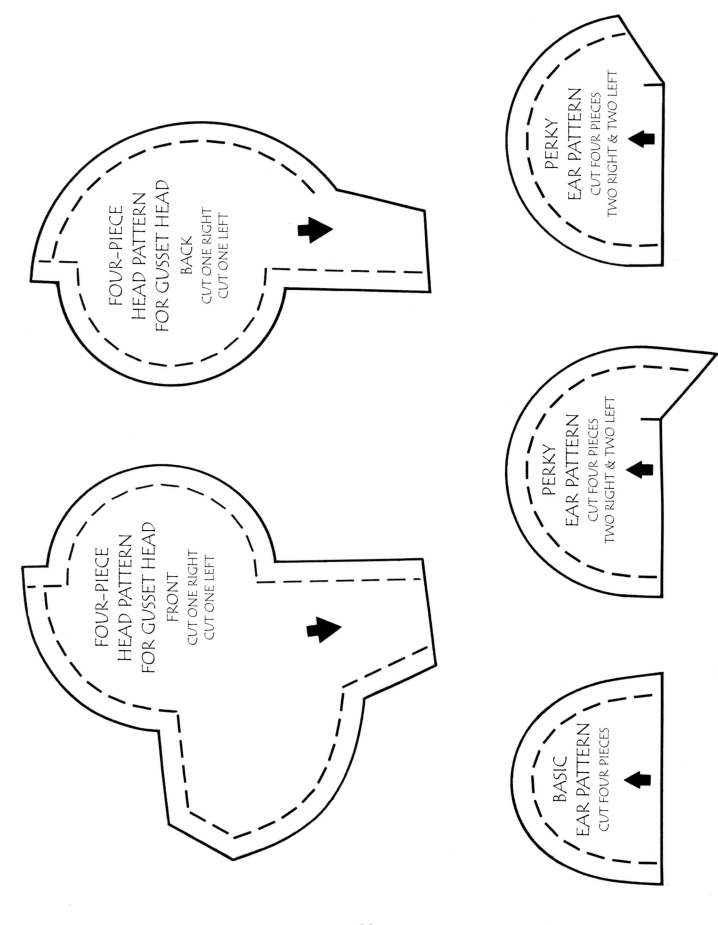

FOUR-PIECE
HEAD PATTERN
FOR GUSSET HEAD
BACK
CUT ONE RIGHT
CUT ONE LEFT

FOUR-PIECE
HEAD PATTERN
FOR GUSSET HEAD
FRONT
CUT ONE RIGHT
CUT ONE LEFT

PERKY
EAR PATTERN
CUT FOUR PIECES
TWO RIGHT & TWO LEFT

PERKY
EAR PATTERN
CUT FOUR PIECES
TWO RIGHT & TWO LEFT

BASIC
EAR PATTERN
CUT FOUR PIECES

86

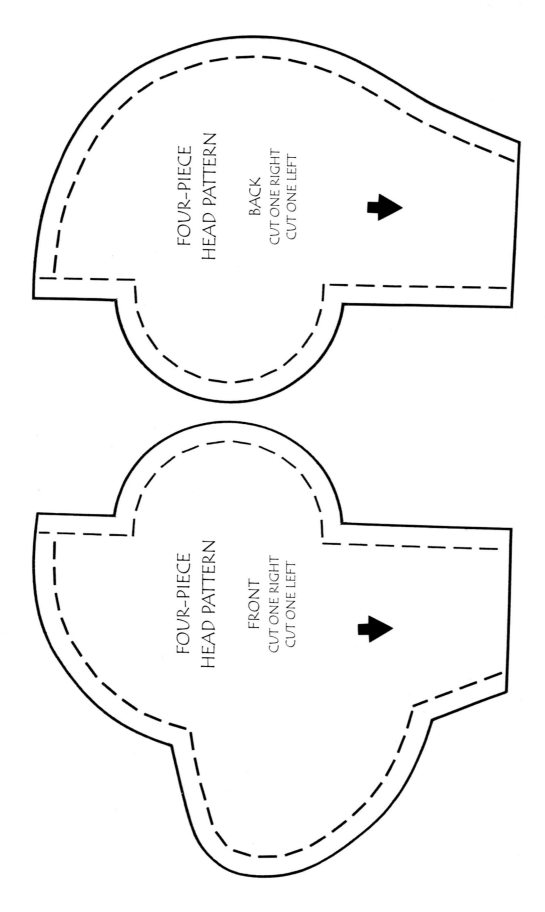

FOUR-PIECE
HEAD PATTERN

BACK
CUT ONE RIGHT
CUT ONE LEFT

FOUR-PIECE
HEAD PATTERN

FRONT
CUT ONE RIGHT
CUT ONE LEFT

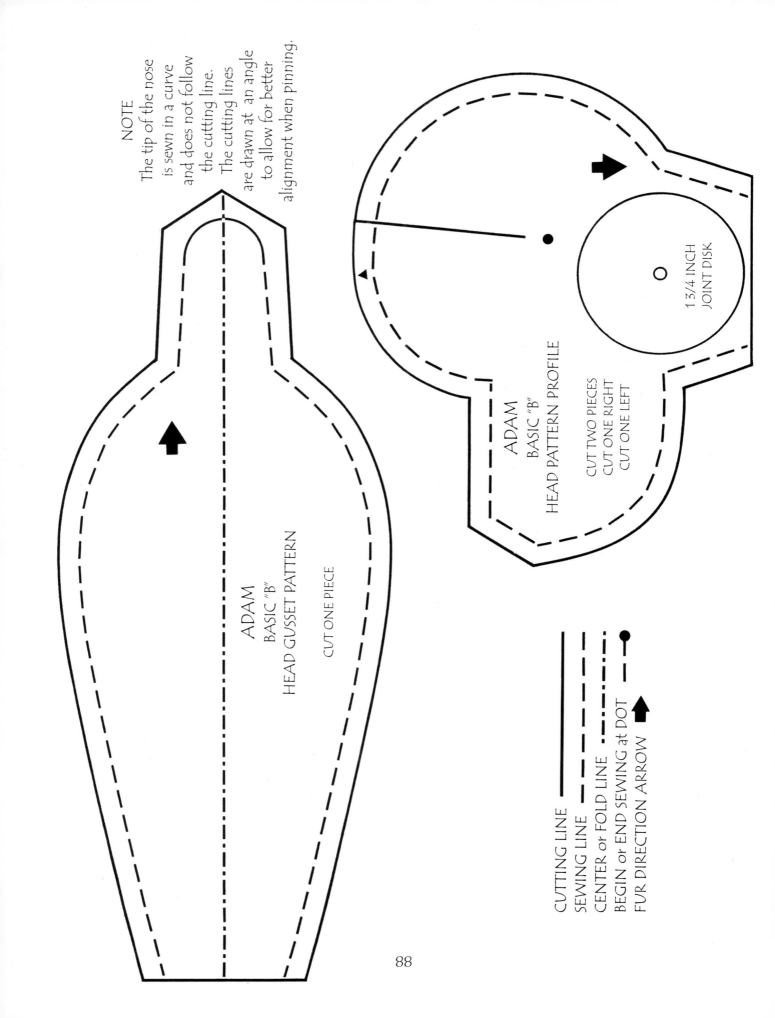

NOTE
The tip of the nose is sewn in a curve and does not follow the cutting line. The cutting lines are drawn at an angle to allow for better alignment when pinning.

ADAM
BASIC "B"
HEAD GUSSET PATTERN

CUT ONE PIECE

ADAM
BASIC "B"
HEAD PATTERN PROFILE

CUT TWO PIECES
CUT ONE RIGHT
CUT ONE LEFT

1 3/4 INCH
JOINT DISK

CUTTING LINE
SEWING LINE
CENTER or FOLD LINE
BEGIN or END SEWING at DOT
FUR DIRECTION ARROW

88

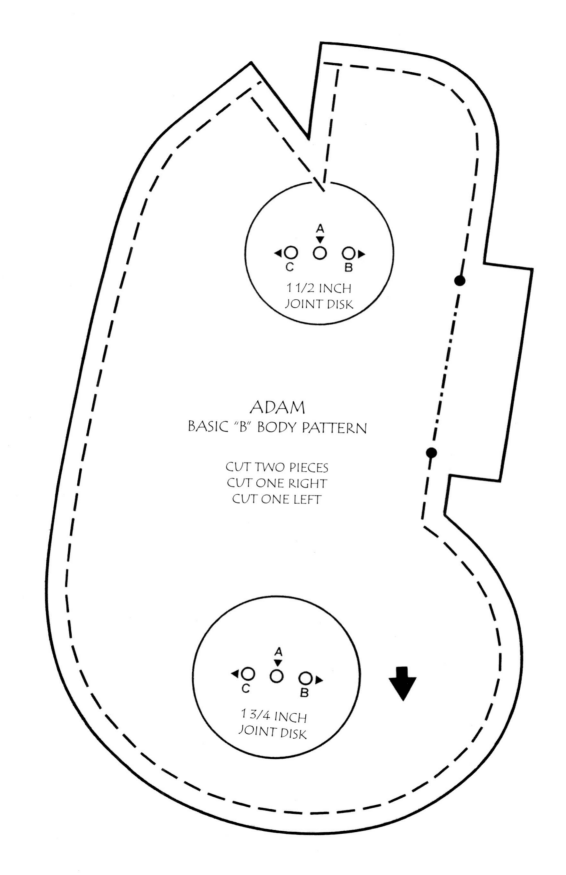

ADAM
BASIC "B" BODY PATTERN

CUT TWO PIECES
CUT ONE RIGHT
CUT ONE LEFT

1 1/2 INCH
JOINT DISK

1 3/4 INCH
JOINT DISK

A

C B

A

C B

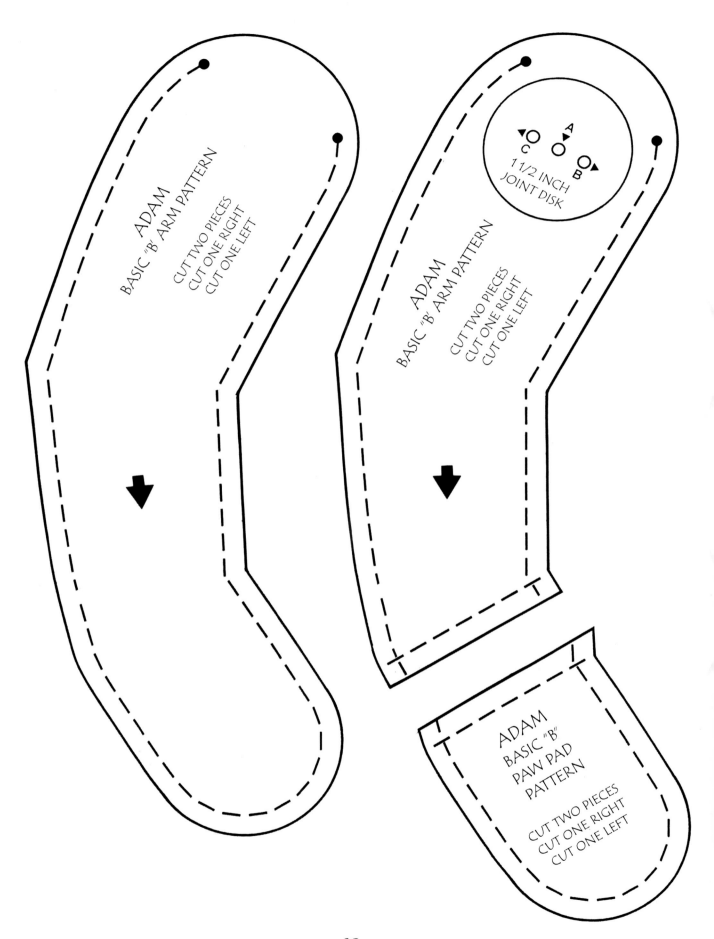

ADAM

BASIC "B" ARM PATTERN

CUT TWO PIECES
CUT ONE RIGHT
CUT ONE LEFT

ADAM

BASIC "B" ARM PATTERN

CUT TWO PIECES
CUT ONE RIGHT
CUT ONE LEFT

A
C
B

1 1/2 INCH
JOINT DISK

ADAM
BASIC "B"
PAW PAD
PATTERN

CUT TWO PIECES
CUT ONE RIGHT
CUT ONE LEFT

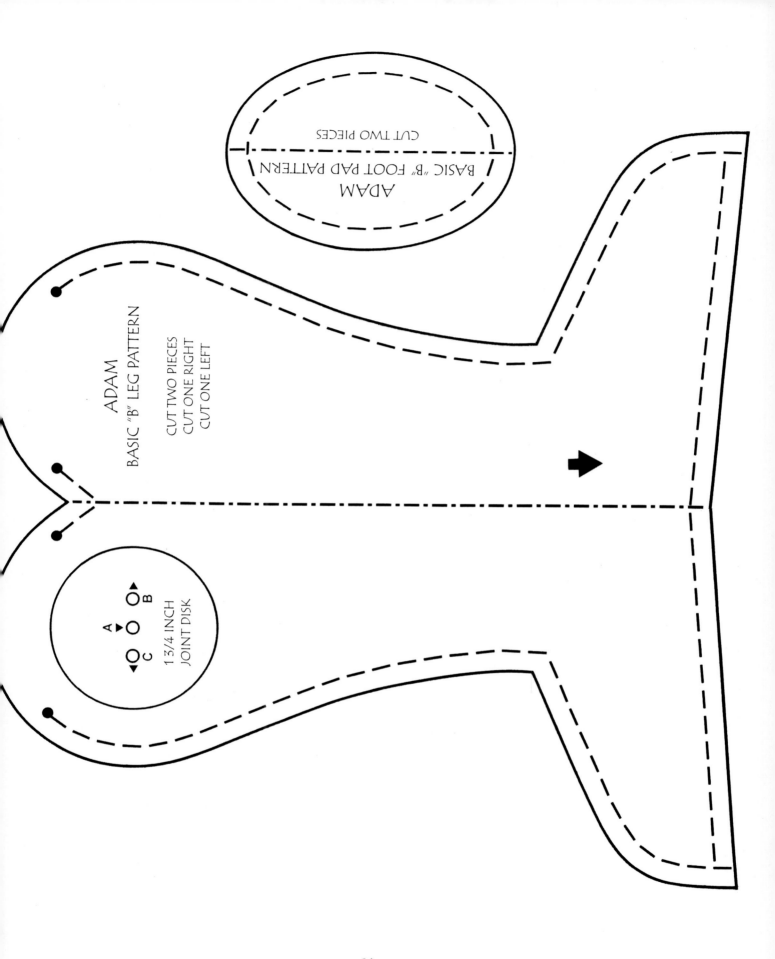

ADAM
BASIC "B" FOOT PAD PATTERN
CUT TWO PIECES

ADAM
BASIC "B" LEG PATTERN

CUT TWO PIECES
CUT ONE RIGHT
CUT ONE LEFT

A
B
C

1 3/4 INCH
JOINT DISK

If you do not dream, you cannot discover
what is beyond your dreams.

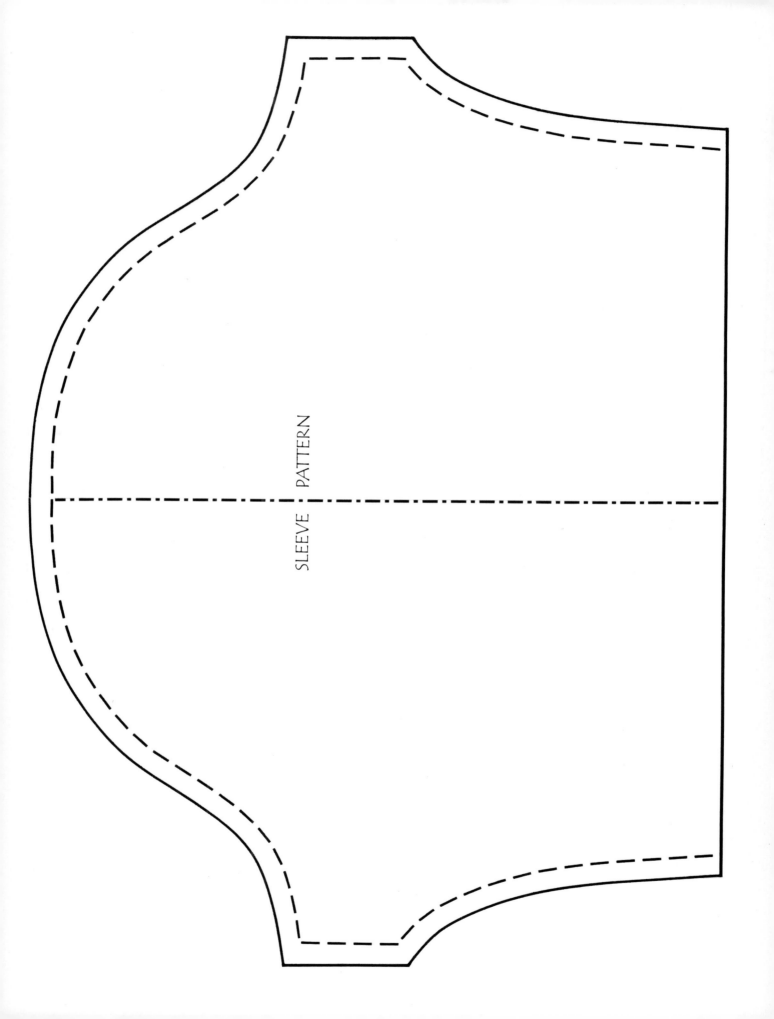

SLEEVE PATTERN

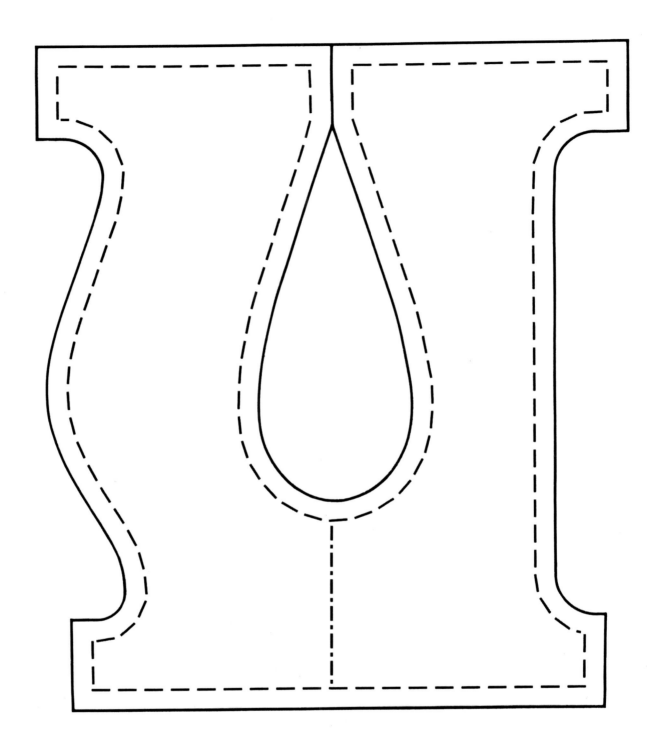

THE BASIC BODICE PATTERN FOR EVE

This is the basic EVE bodice pattern with a scoop neckline and curved cap sleeve. This is the easiest, least complicated, bodice pattern you can make.

The right-hand side of the pattern has the straight line shoulder design that is used for overalls and also as an arm hole when adding a sleeve to the bodice.

By following the simple directions you can alter this pattern to create a number of different outfits for your little Lady Bear.

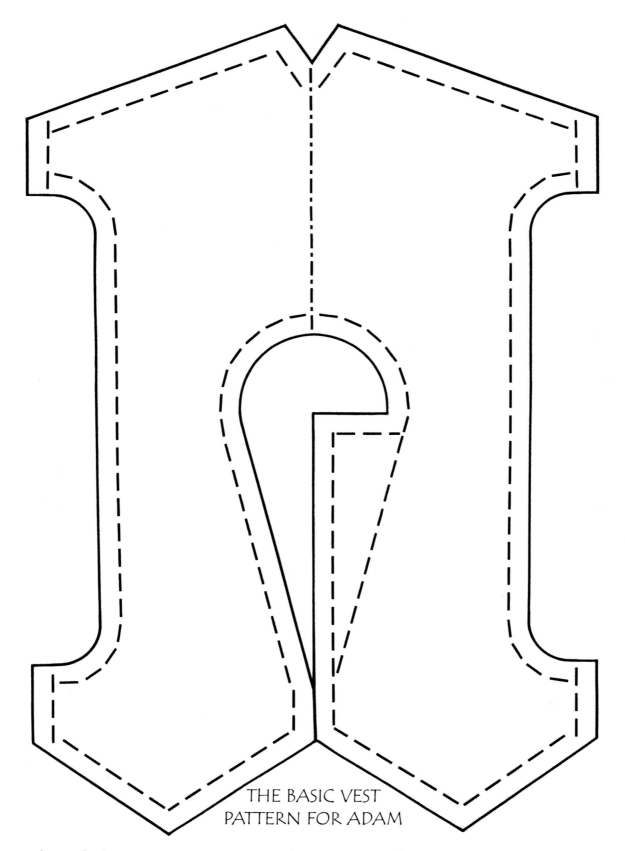

THE BASIC VEST
PATTERN FOR ADAM

This is the basic ADAM vest pattern. This pattern can also be used to create a jacket with sleeves. This is the easiest, least complicated, vest pattern you can make. The right-hand side of the pattern indicates how to add a simple collar flap to the front of the jacket or vest.

By following the simple directions you can alter this pattern to create a number of different outfits for your Gentleman Bear.

TEDDY BEAR PHOTOGRAPHS

All of the bears photographed for this book were created from the basic patterns, or modified variations of those patterns.

Page 1 – "Samantha" was created from the basic EVE pattern with PUPPY ears.
Page 4 – "Crumpet" was created from the basic ADAM pattern with PERKY ears and a modified head pattern (see page 22).
Page 8 – "Flora" was created from the basic EVE pattern with PUPPY ears.
Page 12 – "Rosebud" was created from the basic EVE pattern with PUPPY ears.
Page 14 – "Becky" was created from the basic EVE pattern with BASIC ears.
Page 16 – "Zac" (larger bear) was created from the basic EVE pattern with PUPPY ears. "Scraps" (smaller bear) was created using the simple four-piece head (see page 36).
Page 38 – "Zac" was created from the basic EVE pattern with PUPPY ears..
Page 48 – "Buster" was created from the basic ADAM pattern with PERKY ears.
Page 58 – "BerryBear" was created from the basic EVE pattern with BASIC ears.
Page 64 – "Autumn" was created from the basic EVE pattern with PERKY ears.
Page 65 – "Companion" was created from the basic EVE pattern with PERKY ears and a modified TEEN-AGE TEDDY body pattern (see page 19).
Page 66 – "Taffy" was created from the basic EVE pattern with BASIC ears.
Page 67 – "Strawberry" was created from the basic EVE head pattern with PERKY ears.
Page 68 – "Rascal" was created from the basic EVE head pattern with PERKY ears and a modified TEEN-AGE TEDDY body pattern (see page 19).
Page 69 – "Lady Rose" was created from the TEEN-AGE BEAR pattern variation (see page 21).
Page 70 – "AdoraBelle" was created from the basic EVE pattern.
Page 71 – "CuddleCub" was created from the basic ADAM pattern.
Page 72 – "Elf Queen" was created from the basic EVE head pattern with modified BASIC ears and a neck added (see page 28). The HIGH-FASHION BEAR body (see page 21) had the arms and legs modified by lengthening them (see page 27).
Page 73 – "YellowBird" was created from a modified basic ADAM pattern (see page 22) with BASIC ears.
Page 74 – "Pinky" (left) was created from the basic EVE pattern with PERKY ears. "Brett" (right) was created from the basic ADAM pattern with PERKY ears.
Page 75 – "Pumpkin" (left) was created from the basic ADAM head pattern with PERKY ears and a basic EVE body. "Clover" (right) was created from the basic EVE head pattern with PERKY ears and a basic EVE body.
Page 76 – "BlueBelle" was created from the TEEN AGE BEAR pattern variation (see page 21).
Page 77 – "Bingo" was created from a modified ADAM head pattern (see page 22).
Page 78 – "Winter" was created from the basic EVE pattern with PERKY ears.
Page 79 – "Zac" was created from the basic EVE head pattern with PUPPY ears and a TIMELESS TEDDY body (see page 19).
Page 80 – "Toots" was created from the basic EVE head pattern with PERKY ears and an extended neck (see page 28). The arms were modified as well (see page 27).
Page 81 – "Spring" was created from the basic EVE pattern with PERKY ears.
Page 92 – "Bearzaar Bear" was created from the basic EVE pattern with PERKY ears.